INSTEAD OF THERAPY

RENA WINTERS

Copyright (C) 2021 Rena Winters

Layout design and Copyright (C) 2021 by Next Chapter

Published 2021 by Next Chapter

Edited by Darci Heikkinen

Cover art by CoverMint

This book is a work of fiction. Names, characters, places, and incidents are the product of the author's imagination or are used fictitiously. Any resemblance to actual events, locales, or persons, living or dead, is purely coincidental.

All rights reserved. No part of this book may be reproduced or transmitted in any form or by any means, electronic or mechanical, including photocopying, recording, or by any information storage and retrieval system, without the author's permission.

PREFACE

A life followed through its seasons. A collection of journal entries, brief Christian insights, short stories, reflections, and poetry written over a lifetime. Taken from a diary of daily living by Rena Winters, a noted newspaper columnist and Hollywood film and television writer. Rena Winters has an outstanding record as a writer of TV specials, including "My Little Corner of the World" [winner of the Freedoms Foundation and American Family Heritage Awards]. Writer and co-host with Robert Stack, "How to Change Your Life" [winner of the Angel Award Best Family Special]. Writer for Peter Marshall's show "One More Time." Author of the highly successful book "Smurfs: The Inside Story of the Little Blue Characters." Contributing author to "I Pledge Allegiance."

ACKNOWLEDGEMENT

Special thanks to my husband Robert Cawley for his continued encouragement to complete this book.

Also, thanks to Keith Bettinger for his help in compiling the various documents.

INTRODUCTION
HOLLYWOOD

In the make believe world where nothing is as it seems,
I have spent my life, my years of toll and dreams.
The city with its sign on high waiting for actors
And actresses to pass by.

I built a life way up in the sky
Where everything is perfect in my office in the sky.
A home away from home, where I compose
What they call prose for movies and television.

As fate would dictate
The money is great.
My treadmill life of duty
Persists in pursuit of fame and beauty.

Endless 18 hour days
Seem to fade into a haze
As I wonder through each project
Creating half crazed.

INTRODUCTION

There is no time for pleasure or reruns
Only work and ratings are considered fun.
One day all of this will be over and
I will return home to roll in the clover.

But for now it is a most exciting high
And I cannot walk away and say goodbye.

SPRING

WARM WELCOME OF SPRING

It's the season for which everyone waits—poets and plumbers, little kids and lovers. Nature gives us an often surprising mix of sun, rain, winds, warmth, and chill. April is unlike any other month in that respect. It's the season of renewal, rebirth.

It's also a good time for rededication—think of those things we've been promising ourselves to do and then do them. Get out a pen and make a list of much-delayed tasks—letters to write, old folks and friends to visit, those nice things you've meant to do for others. They'll mean so much to someone, and you'll feel better for doing them. Spring is the season for growth of a very personal nature—so bring on the warmth.

SPRING INTERLUDE

This is the morning of the year,
With fresh, pink painted sunrise,
And dewdrops like a fairy's tear
To make each morn a lovely prize.
Lie down upon the pulsing ground
Beneath a lacy tree.

Look up and up until you've found
The sky....blue as can be.
Watch a bird on lazy wing
Soaring far above
Listen to the crickets sing
Of spring.... of joy.... of love.

SPRINGTIME IN THE MOUNTAINS

Springtime is a wonderful time to renew and rejuvenate our lives and our thinking. Just as all of nature's creations began life in the springtime, it's time to begin life anew. To stretch and broaden and widen our horizons and our thinking. To burst forth with flowers of love to all those around us. To everyone and everything we touch.

Dear Lord, I pray that we may capture and hold on to that wonderful feeling of springtime in our hearts all year through, and there's absolutely no reason why we shouldn't. If we would only praise our Lord and stop a moment each day to give thanks to him. The next time you see a fresh cut flower, stop for just a moment and say a silent prayer to God, thanking him for allowing each of us to be formed in his image and yet allowing each of us the freedom to be individuals. Thank him also for the beauty and love that he surrounds us with each day.

A SPRING THOUGHT

One morning I awakened at dawn and realized that a door had closed in my life. I know that each of you has had a door close in your life at some time. I lingered by that closed door, then, as in previous losses, I walked alone.

The wet grass beneath my feet healed my body, the trees overhead fed my spirit, and I kept hearing or thought I heard, "Live it now; you cannot live tomorrow unless you live today, this moment." Then I became aware of the great process of time; we hold nothing. All things go. I became a part of that great stream of time when the ancient life forms started. I could see those life forms as though in progression, vivid as a chart on a museum wall. Yet the ancient hieroglyphics speak only of today, and an unbelievable optimism overflowed me. The life force moves. It continues to grow and change. It re-creates from decaying hearts new grasses—perhaps in a different form, and there is an expanding consciousness to perceive the wonder of this movement of life. Suddenly, I knew my part in this. It was not to war with progress, not to spend my force grieving because the buffalo are gone and the whale may be leaving, not grasping for some utopian future, but from my thought and feeling, first in mind and heart and then in words to tell what it is, just what it is, this day.

So, this wonderful spring day, I saw a blossom in a tree; it bloomed high above the branches, bursting forth with brilliant color. I saw the arched head of a deer, the gentle grace of a doe in movement; I saw a cottontail, standing as a statue. For a while, I walked in the tracks of a raccoon. I sat on a moss-covered stump and wondered what myth am I living? Promptly the answer came, it is the miracle of God at work, and the words came rushing in my head clearly, "The Lord is my Shepherd. I shall not want. He maketh me to lie down in green pastures. He leadeth me beside the still waters. He restoreth my soul. He leadeth me in the paths of righteousness for his name's sake. Yea, though I walk through the valley of the shadow of death, I will fear no evil; for thou art with me; thy rod and thy staff, they comfort me. Thou preparest a table before me in the presence of mine enemies; thou anointest my head with oil; my cup runneth over. Surely goodness and mercy shall follow me all the days of my life, and I will dwell in the house of the Lord forever.

I departed the woods and went to the beach. Through cracks in the pier, there includes from my eyes, I saw two swallows with golden-lined beaks closed in their carefully feathered nest. They slept the deep sleep of infant's sleep; their elders sat on the dock rail, chatting together before starting the day of feeding their young. I heard the call of a heron and the splash of the dive of a gull. I listened to all the birds and the wonderful sounds of the ocean.

On this day, I walked in the good earth, the dirt, and the sand. I smelled the clean, fresh air of the mountains and the cool salt air of the sea. I saw a blossom high in a tree, and it healed me. I heard myself saying, "Let the past go, let the future be; it is enough to feel, and see, and be in this instant in time."

I understand that the door was not really closed; all the life and love I had known walked with me beneath the trees. Life flows in an endless stream and being a part of life, we flow with it. Spring has many faces, like a beautiful woman whose features fragment in the ripples of a stream; there are two faces of spring that I hold very dear although they are at opposite sides of nature's spectrum.

Have you ever spent a springtime afternoon in San Francisco ... that Bagdad by the bay? You will see lovely girls in bright spring dresses ... handsome, tanned men, and the orange paint of that famous bridge silhouetted against the sky. And on the hills, the skyscrapers, towers, and cathedrals—awe-inspiring canyons of steel that give testimony to man's great creative genius.

All of this is just the window dressing for God's wonder that is spring. The winds of March drive frothy white caps across the bay, and in the bright blue sky, the soft white clouds skid and speed over the heavens to the final rendezvous with the golden sunset. Another face of spring can be seen in the hill country. You know spring comes in many ways to many places, but she must love the mountains the best because it is here the first buds appear on the trees while the winter snow still clings to the ground below. It is here that a riot of wildflowers first comes to bloom, and the roaring river seems to sing an anthem to the coming of spring ... the rebirth of the land. This is the prelude to the lush dark green of summer, the age-old promise given at the beginning of time, God's spring, blossoms, soft breezes, and butterflies, the all-enveloping peace and serenity. This is springtime in the mountain.

Springtime is a wonderful time to renew and rejuvenate

our lives and our thinking. Just as all of nature's creations began life in the springtime. It's time to begin life anew, to stretch and broaden and widen our horizons and our thinking. To burst forth with flowers of love to all those around us, to everyone and everything we touch.

VALENTINES

Webster's dictionary describes love as a strong affection or liking for someone or something.

Love of God—a spiritual love, to cherish someone very special and hope that we can attain a little of that consciousness.

Love of self—a seeking to uplift our lives.

Love for husband or wife. Man or woman.

Someone to share a lifetime with. Someone to share thoughts and ideas with—to share responsibilities and joys, to look forward to years of happiness, to enjoy sexual pleasures with. Someone to raise children with.

Love for children—cherish each one in a special way, recognizing each of their talents and gifts, encouraging them when they fail, and most of all hoping that they far surpass us in their lifetimes. Hoping that they achieve a successful marriage and happy family lives, that they have a rewarding career, that they are endowed with a great love and understanding and respect for all things Godly—religious.

Love for a friend—someone who supports us in times of

tragedy and sadness. Someone who we can accept exactly as they are and admire them for being themselves. Someone who will always give an honest answer when we seek it.

Love for a pet —animal, bird, or whatever.

Something to care for, to watch their growth, help in their development—for a pet loves us, for just being us. They are dependent on us, but we don't mind because they give so much affection in return.

Love for humanity, love for a brother and sister. We grow up learning to love our brothers and sisters because they are family members. Although when we are young, we sometimes wonder if they are really necessary in our lives. We grew up loving them because they are a part of us. A blood relation.

But love for all humanity takes a bit of doing. To look at some of the people in the world today and say I truly love you like a brother is sometimes very difficult to do. Yet, if you look beyond the exterior, the dirty clothes, the uncouth qualities, the environment, you will see a truly beautiful person.

For even the worse criminal has some redeeming quality about him. If we but look for it. It may be that they love their mother or father, cherish a wife or child, or have a lasting friendship with someone special. There is something.

They are not all bad. For no one is truly all bad. Circumstances, life, environment, past lives, and karma all play a role in a person's development, be it for good or bad. The important thing is, if our own viewpoint is centered on love for humanity, we will overlook the bad and see only the good.

Know that you know what love is; let's look at what love is not.

It is not unforgiveness, resentment, ill will, bearing a grudge, malice, retaliation, hostility, bitterness, hatred, or never forgetting something.

I want you to concentrate and think about your own lives ...

are you guilty of one of the above? If so, this minute, now, confess to God your failing, confess your faith, and take steps to permanently put these words and actions out of your life forever. Bluntly, you don't need them.

Not ever again will you fall into this trap, for you are taking steps from now on toward becoming a loving person. Toward love ... and if we become a loving person, we will in return become loved.

The Bible says love is of God. And God is love.

As we approach Valentine's Day, remember God's commandment that we should love one and another ... and take direct action to love our enemies. That's right, you can do it. Love your enemies. Cherish your friends. Tell your family they are special. Express it in words and actions. Spread love, joy, happiness, and a smile to all you come in contact with.

Don't be depressed if you are alone because if you remember God's commandment to love one and another and truly work at being a loving person, you will know God loves you. You will find someone, somehow, somewhere to share a part of the day.

LADY

Although I conquer all the earth,
Yet for me there is only one city.
In that city there is only one house,
And in that house, one room only,
And in that room, a bed
And one woman sleeps there.
The shining joy and jewel of all my kingdom.

UNKNOWN LADY

There is a toast that I want to share to the woman I'll never know,
To the woman who's going to take my place, when it's time for me to go.
I've wondered what kind of lady she'll be; I've wished I could take her hand
just to whisper, I wish you well woman, in a way that she would understand.
I'd like to give her the cheering word that I've longed at times to hear
I'd like to give her the warm hand clasp, when never a friend seems near.
I've learned my knowledge by sheer hard work, and I wish I could pass it on,
to the woman who comes to take my place, the day when I will be gone.
Will she see all the mistakes I have made and note all the battles lost?

Will she ever guess of the tears they caused, or the heart aches which they cost?
Will she gaze through the failures and fruitless toil, to the underlying plan?
And catch a glimpse of the real intent, and the heart of the vanquished woman?
I dare to hope she may pause someday as she toils as I have wrought
and gains some strength for her task, from the battles I have fought.
But I've only the task itself to leave, with the cares for her to face, and never a casual word may speak, to the woman who'll take my place.
Then here's to your health my friend, I toast you as a bridegroom to a bride.
I leave an unfinished task for you, but God knows that I've tried. I've dreamed my dreams as all women do, but only a few came true, and my hope today is that all the dreams may be realized in you.
We'll meet someday in the great unknown, out in the realm of space,
you'll know my clasp as I take your hand, and gaze into your face.
Then all failures will be successes, in the light of the new found dawn.
So I am toasting your health my friend, to the lady who'll take my place when I am gone.

THE LEGEND OF ST. VALENTINE

The story of Valentine's Day begins in the third century with an oppressive Roman emperor and a humble Christian martyr. The emperor was Claudius II. The Christian was Valentinus.

Claudius had ordered all Romans to worship twelve gods, and he had made it a crime punishable by death to associate with Christians. But Valentinus was dedicated to the ideals of Christ, and not even the threat of death could keep him from preaching his beliefs. He was arrested and imprisoned.

During the last weeks of Valentinus's life, a remarkable thing happened. Seeing that he was a man of learning, the jailer asked whether his daughter, Julia, might be brought to Valentinus for lessons. She had been blind since birth. Julia was a pretty young girl with a quick mind. Valentinus read stories of Rome's history to her. He described the world of nature to her. He taught her arithmetic and told her about God. She saw the world through his eyes, trusted in his wisdom, and found comfort in his quiet strength.

"Valentinus, does God really hear our prayers?" Julia asked one day.

"Yes, my child. He hears each one," he replied.

"Do you know what I pray for every morning and every night? I pray that I might see. I want so much to see everything you've told me about!"

"God does what is best for us if we will only believe in him," Valentinus said.

"Oh, Valentinus, I do believe," Julia said intensely. "I do." She knelt and grasped his hand.

They sat quietly together, each praying. Suddenly, there was a brilliant light in the prison cell. Radiant, Julia screamed. "Valentinus, I can see! I can see!"

"Praise be to God!" Valentinus exclaimed, and he knelt in prayer. On the eve of his death, Valentinus wrote a last note to Julia, urging her to stay close to God, and he signed it "From Your Valentine." His sentence was carried out the next day, February 14, 270, near a gate that was later named Porta Valentini in his memory. He was buried at what is now the Church of Prasedes in Rome. It is said that Julia herself planted a pink blossom almond tree near his grave. Today, the almond tree remains a symbol of abiding love and friendship. On each February 14th, St. Valentine's Day, messages of affection, love, and devotion are exchanged around the world.

WOMAN, THE GREAT INFLUENCER

Sharing equally with love in the capacity to influence, the fates saw fit to include in their intricate design another great disturber—WOMAN.

Brilliant and luminous—sinister and black. The career of women in history is akin to a flaming torch whirling through the darkness.

The center of intrigue, plot, and conspiracy, the power behind the throne, the inspiration for achievement, the tool, the instigator, the foil, the despoiler, the pawn, the reward, the cause, the effect, the beginning, the end—this is the history of woman.

Thus, woman stands out, illuminating an otherwise dark picture. Sometimes magnificent, sometimes great, leaving an imperishable, immortal record.

The molder of destiny, the creator of history.

LOVE, THE GREAT DISTURBER

No general outline of history, however sketchy, would be complete without a tribute to that capricious, whimsical, tragic little god that the glamorous ages of mythology gave us: CUPID—god of love.

Nor may any outline of history be written without tracing the effect of this dynamic emotion upon the lives of men, of dynasties, of empires.

Love of power, love of wealth, love of glory, love of woman or man. In these broad human terms are the flaming pages of history written.

On the darker pages of the book, the byproducts of love —malice, envy, hatred, cruelty, avarice, jealousy, suspicion—recorded in blood and fire and war; that ceaseless struggle of man in his pilgrimage from obscurity to a place in the sun.

FAIRY GODMOTHER

Today, we are going to take a trip back to our childhood. Pretend that you are young once again and remember with me the magical fairy Godmother who was talked about so often in our children's books, Cinderella and other children's fairy tales. Our fairy Godmother could grant any wish with just a sweep of her magical wand. Pretend now that you are holding that magical wand. See it in your hand. Now wave that wand as a musical conductor would do. Look about you; the room is ablaze with dazzling lights. The chairs, the tables are prismatic crystals, sparkling with a thousand shades of red, yellow, green, and blue ... colors such as you have never seen before. Your clothes are shinning and glittery also. They are shining as if on fire with a million tiny flames. The colors of ruby, emerald, and sapphire.

The air itself sparks as if millions of miniature meteors are darting all about you. In another wave of your wand, we hear a hurricane of sound. The playing of a hundred-piece symphony orchestra. Every object in the room is booming, resonating, or thrilling to the most complex form of music. The colors I have described and the sounds I have described—that you are now visualizing—are with us every day. They are above and below the small octave that is perceivable by human senses. In a sense, we are surrounded by millions of atoms so microscopic that we cannot see them. We are surrounded each day with zillions of sound waves that we cannot hear. Just stop quietly now and see if you can hear any sounds in the silence. Force your closed eyes to see beyond what they normally can see.

Concentrate deeply; know that you can see through your third eye. Through closed eyes, many blind people have proven that vision is possible beyond our ordinary senses. Stop and listen. Can you hear the sounds? Force your ears to hear sounds that they would not normally hear.

Know that you can do it.

NIGHTS

Nights are growing very lonely,
Days are very long.
I'm growing weary only
Listening for your song.

Old remembrances are thronging
Through my memory.
Till it seems the world is full of dreams
Just to call you back to me.

All night long I hear you calling
Calling sweet and low.
Seem to hear your footsteps falling,
Everywhere I go.

Though the round between us stretches
Many a weary mile
I forget that you're not with me yet.
When I think I see you smile.

BLACK KNIGHT

My Black Knight comes to me in the night
He appears as a vision, clear and bold and strong
Then becomes cloudy and he doesn't stay long

My Black Knight appears in the day
At awkward moments he flashes a smile, a motion
But then he fades away and doesn't stay.

Is it really all smoke and mirrors?
Can I cheer? Or is he a figment of my imagination
Something I create to fulfill my empty situation.

My Black Knight is so strong,
so wonderful how can it be wrong? No matter what,
I'm going to make the adventure prolong.

One day I may have to say so long.
For now I will cling to my vision
With time, tenacity and precision.

ENDURING HAPPINESS

Take two heaping cups of patience
1 heart full of love
2 handfuls of generosity
Dash of laughter
1 headful of understanding
Sprinkle generously with kindness.

Enduring happiness is not a commodity that can be bought from without. It is the sublimation of what you have to give from within. Human happiness is not derived from material wealth so much as from intellectual, moral, and spiritual health. That enduring happiness can be secured from constant study, reading, traveling, and varied interests in life. Good books, fine periodicals and reviews, good friends, affection of loved ones, plenty of outdoor fun, relaxation and recreation, laughter, and a wholesome environment are essential items that sustain abiding happiness, joy, and health.

ELIZABETH FRY

Through the years, Christian women have played major roles in bringing the word of God to the peoples of all lands. One prime example was Elizabeth Fry, who accomplished greater prison reforms than any other woman in history. Kings asked for her counsel, and her influence spread through the world.

Elizabeth Gurney was born in 1780 in Norwich, England —the fourth of twelve children. Her life was that of any other growing child until she turned seventeen years old. At that time, she experienced a tremendous spiritual illumination that was to guide her destiny for the rest of her life.

In 1800 she married Joseph Fry, a member of a prominent and wealthy family. However, society life was not for Elizabeth, for at this time, she started on a lifetime career of prison reform.

It was at the infamous Newgate prison in London where iron doors first clanged shut behind her, sending her into a world of wild beasts. This was virtually true.

Three hundred women and numerous children were crowded into four small rooms that reeked of filth. They were without beds, bedding, or extra clothing and no type of employment.

Removing her bonnet, Elizabeth took a seat facing the prisoners and opened her Bible. To the women in this dark, cold, damp room, she must have seemed a heavenly vision. She turned to the verses in Isaiah 52: 6-7, "All we like sheep have gone astray; we have turned every one to his own way; and the Lord hath laid on him the iniquity of us all. He was oppressed, and he was afflicted, yet he opened not his mouth."

Elizabeth Fry wasted no time after seeing the conditions that the prisoners lived under. First of all, the cells were cleaned and kept clean. Next, she opened a classroom for the children of inmates. Soon she found all sorts of materials to provide employment, and she was instrumental in having the first matron hired in Newgate history.

She succeeded because she knew how to apply Christianity to her problems and because she was willing to labor on with patience and indomitable perseverance month after month, year after year.

In addition to prison reforms in all of Europe and the United States, Elizabeth Fry was a prime mover of a variety of organizations that provided food and shelter to the homeless and jobs for the unemployed. She also organized libraries and started the pioneer institution for the training of nurses in England.

In addition, Mrs. Fry was a successful wife and mother. She had eight children, and seven of those children bore biblical names.

When Frederick William IV, King of Prussia, came to England for the christening of the infant Prince of Wales, the King asked to visit Newgate prison with Mrs. Fry. In his presence, she read to the prisoners the twelfth chapter of

Romans. "So we, being many, are one body in Christ, and every one members one of another."

When she knelt, the King followed her example and listened attentively to her beautiful, extemporaneous prayer. The scene was a moving one. The monarch of a great nation, dignitaries of England, and prisoners all praying to their common creator.

Elizabeth Fry died on October 12, 1845. Her last words were: "I can say one thing, since my heart was touched at seventeen by God; I believe I never have awakened from sleep in sickness or in health, by day or by night, without my first waking thought being how I might best serve my Lord."

COLORS

The study of color phenomena is the most interesting of all the physical sciences. This is because colors are something that can be seen with the naked eye, and while their physical characteristics cannot readily be felt by most people as a skin sensation, their ability to produce physical changes will readily become apparent.

Colors influence your everyday life, and if you wish them to affect you favorably, you will study your color needs and supply those needs as carefully as you supply your dietary needs. The person using color therapy deals with the physical aspects of color as related to disease and applies these colors to change disease vibrations into healing vibrations.

Each color is different to your eye because each color vibrates differently. This vibration power of color is perhaps one of our greatest physical phenomena. The usage of color should be done with an abundant amount of extreme caution and knowledge. It's better to use less exposure than to overexpose one to certain color vibrations.

We will be dealing with the following colors: red, orange,

yellow, green, and blue. We will correlate the colors with the colors of the force centers of your body, the chakras.

For those of you who are not familiar with the term chakras, they are the nerve centers of power as taught in Hatha yoga. First at the base of the spine, at the level of the genital organs, in the area of the navel, around the heart, in the throat, and at the forehead. When one has advanced sufficiently, they are said to have awakened kundalini. The vital force that flows through the interior of the spinal cord awakening the chakras and sensitizing them so that physic powers are attained.

The first color to examine is red. The wavelength of red is 1/133,000 of an inch, and its rate of vibration is 437 trillion times per second. Red is an excellent color, at nearly the center of heat. Red stimulates and energizes and is closely correlated with the physical body. Red is the force of germination. Reproduction, building up of form, and the creative power of all nature. It has a stimulating effect on the mind and body as it increases the activity of arterial blood flow.

Red stimulates certain centers of the body, causing the adrenal supply to the ductless glands to be released into the bloodstream. It also stimulates the formation of hemoglobin and corpuscles, and increased energy is thus attained. The temperature is raised, circulation increases in the system, and the body is tuned in general. Red is attuned to the first chakra of the body at the sacral base (the kundalini).

Orange. The orange color is formed by a blending of reds and yellows. Orange is the color of change. Used in changing things for the better. Orange vibrates at 506 trillion times per second. Orange and red work closely together. Orange works on the adrenal system as well as the red. It also has a powerful influence on the liver and on the elimination process of the body. It helps to govern the pancreas and sugar metabolism. It can also successfully help to treat other conditions such as inflammation of the kidneys, gall stones, and cessation of menstruation, along with mental depression. Orange is related to the second force center of the body or the spleen chakra.

Yellow. Yellow vibrates 535 trillion times per second. Yellow stimulates the brain as well as exerting significant therapeutic influences on the assimilative organs of the body. It stimulates the purifying action of the body. It has a large effect upon the liver, gall bladder, and intestines, thus aiding in the elimination of the body as well as its cleansing action. Yellow improves the texture of the skin, healing scars and other blemishes. Yellow can be used successfully on stomach troubles, indigestion, constipation, and flatulence (gas), liver trouble, diabetes, nervous exhaustion, and can give quick energy. Yellow is attuned to the third chakra of the solar plexus.

Green. Green vibrates at 577 trillion times per second. Green brings soothing effects over an individual and upon the nervous system. Green is formed by using the colors yellow and blue. Green has been useful in affecting one's blood pressure and in the alleviation of headaches, neuralgia, influenza, and syphilis. It will significantly influence in breaking down inharmonious vibrations of malignant growths and helping to tune up the nervous system to bring about greater harmony within and without one's own being. The color green is to the spiritual life what food and water are to the physical. As these elements nourish our bodies, so does color nourish the soul and the spirit. Green is attuned to the fourth chakra or the heart chakra.

Blue. Blue works on a wavelength of 1/57,000 of an inch and vibrates at 658 trillion times per second. Blue successfully combats fever conditions, bleeding, germs, nervous irritation, thyroid, cholera, various poxes, measles, apoplexy, hysteria, and epilepsy. It stimulates the flow of iodine from the thyroid gland. Blue is used to produce quicker growth of vegetables, and it also enhances the flavor of eggs. It is an excellent balance for the body. The color blue also has a spiritual quality with high religious devotion. Blue is attuned to the fifth chakra or the throat area.

The foregoing colors are the primary shades you should have knowledge of. I would like to mention two extremely strong colors. Violet affects the crown chakra and indigo, which affects the third eye. Both of these are very powerful in developing physic intuitiveness.

Years ago, there used to be a superstition that colors were merely lucky or unlucky. But it has now been proven that colors produce vibrations and, either directly or in combination with music, can be used to help with therapy in hospitals and mental asylums. Their significance in home and office decoration and in clothing should always be borne in mind.

Go on; color correct your world like you would your television set. Improve it. Make it work for you. Become the person that you want to be.

THE WORLD AS A MIRROR

The time has come for you and me to stop blaming the world, the other person, the employer, the employee, the politician, the businessman, the social worker, and so on endlessly for our problems. Every crisis that we face, moment to moment, day to day, has sprung up before us because it is a true reflection of our soul.

The world is the mirror of your soul. Every thought and feeling that flows through you shapes and aligns the direction of the minutest particle of your being and those around you. The very place you sit at this moment, absorbing the content of these words, reflects your soul. The entire world mirrors you. Your general or specific mood, your dreams and visions, or lack of them, your apathy or consciously directed motion, form the very roads beneath your feet, the skies overhead.

TODAY

I've shut the door on yesterday and its sorrows and mistakes. I've locked within its gloomy walls past failures and heartaches. And now I've thrown the key away to seek another room;

I'll furnish it with hope and smiles and every springtime bloom. No thought shall enter this abode that has a hint of pain and every malice and distrust shall never therein reign.

I've shut the door on yesterday and thrown the key away. Tomorrow holds no doubt for me since I have found today.

PERFECT WORLD

A perfect world just can't exist, the folks who know
 will say.
And sometimes things just seem to go from bad to
 worse each day.
But there's a world, a lovely world, as vast as love is
 wide.
Where hopes can leap up to the sky and faith stays at
 high tide.
What world is that, you well might ask? I'd love to
 journey there.
That world is deep inside us all. We live in it through
 prayer.

PASSION FLOWER

The passion flower is the State Flower of Tennessee. If you have never heard the legend about it, you do not enjoy this lovely flower as you might.

The legend relates that each part of the flower is associated with the life of Jesus. There are ten colored parts (including petals and sepals). They represent the ten apostles present at the crucifixion. Peter and Judas being absent. In the center, there are a large number of filaments that represent the crown of thorns. (Another legend considers this as representing the halo about Christ's head.) There are five stamens, which suggest the five wounds he received; one through each hand and foot and one in the side.

The three sections of the pistil typify the three nails; one through each hand and one through both feet. The stamens and pistil are borne upon a column which may be compared to the one to which Jesus was tied when He was scourged. In some species, the leaves are three-parted and represent the Trinity. In others, the leaves are five-parted, which represent the fingers of the hands of persecutors. Since the plant is a tendril-bearing climber, the tendrils represent the whips with which Jesus was scourged.

Hopefully, knowing the above will help you enjoy this beautiful flower more.

PRESIDENT'S DAY

This past week, I found it difficult not to think about the President's holiday that we are soon celebrating. Lincoln was an outstanding President. Noted for being extremely fair-minded. Washington, of course, the Father of our Country certainly was a man of vision.

And my thoughts wandered to other countries I had visited. I remembered one day standing atop the Acropolis, a fortified hill in Athens, Greece, looking at the proud columned ruins of the Parthenon. One of the most magnificent of man's architectural creations. The Parthenon was a Doric, which was a Greek religious temple design centuries ago.

As I stood before it, I overhead an American Marine comment, "I suppose the day will come when others will walk up the great stone steps to the ruins of the American White House, and they will say, 'Here once was a great civilization.'"

At Byblos, one of the oldest of the Middle East's many cities, one can stand and look through seven thousand years of history. One civilization built on the ruins of the last. There, one sees the Stone Age and the civilizations of the Egyptians, the Phoenicians, the Babylonians, the Assyrians, the Greeks, the Arabs, the Romans, the Crusaders, and the Turks. One after another, through seven thousand years, empires rose and then fell from power.

Our history books speak of such colonial empires as Spain and Portugal in the Western hemisphere. I know my grandmother, who came from Spain, would say, "Don't forget in the past we ruled the world" and "Stand up straight, remember your manners, and act like a lady." None of which, as a child, I wanted to hear. However, at one time, Spain was a very powerful country and now, has greatly slipped from power. The Netherlands once ruled in the Far East, and France once controlled Indochina. We have witnessed the decline of the British Empire, upon which it was once said, with understandable pride, "that the sun had never set on the British Empire."

Today, our nation, the USA, stamps its influence on world affairs. Mankind marvels at the technology that has put a man on the moon and that probes into the far reaches of the solar system. Countries marvel at our wealth, our merchandise, our free institutions, and our power.

And we, too, marvel and take pride in the works of our hands. We listen to the call of comfort. The allure of leisure, the demands and pleasures of power.

Better that we should listen thoughtfully to the wind that whispers sadly through the ruins of the Parthenon and observe the eternal stars that wink knowingly over the mounds of ancient cities. No nation is stronger than the ideals upon which it was built.

One nation. Are we really one nation, divided up into states, with different problems, different approaches to solving problems, to rectifying situations? For instance, such as allocation of funds for various projects. Why should some states have better medical programs for their people than others? Why should some states have better school programs than others? Perhaps it would be better if these things were considered on a national basis.

Under God. So much of our country today does not honor God. Or even acknowledge his existence. Much of our country is being purchased by foreigners with different ideals, different religious beliefs. They will begin to affect our national thinking. Our economic planning and those with no religious beliefs certainly will—and do now—affect our country's moral standing. Frequently people with no religious beliefs are those that also do not honor any laws or practice acceptable standards of behavior.

Indivisible. I wonder, today we see riots in the streets. Various protests of all types. Are we trying to ban together or separate those that do not agree with us? Aren't we really dividing instead of multiplying? We should be multiplying.

Radical, yes, I am, about the United States being the greatest.

Angry, yes, about what I see going on. Protests, anti-American tolerance. Worried yes, because I love my country.

American, yes, and very proud of it.

A NATION OF BELIEF

Blessed is the nation whose God is the Lord, and the people whom he hath chosen for his own inheritance.

Our country was founded on its belief in God. In the summer of 1776, delegates from thirteen colonies met to consider the future of their new country. Suggestion after suggestion was offered and rejected. Finally, the discouraged delegates turned to Benjamin Franklin for his opinion. Hesitating a moment, he slowly rose and delivered a brief but powerful message based on Psalms 127 "Except the Lord build the house, they labor in vain; except the Lord keep the city, the watchman waketh but in vain." He suggested a time of prayer. A spirit of unity resulted, and the Declaration of Independence was written. As the liberty bell rang for the first time in Independence Hall, it proclaimed the birth of the United States of America on July 4, 1776.

Eighty-seven years later, during a time of great crisis, President Lincoln in his famous Gettysburg Address, challenged the people of America to resolve "That this nation, under God, shall have a new birth of freedom - and that government of the people, by the people, for the people shall not perish from the earth." There are forces at work today which are trying to take away this freedom. These enemies are strong. Unless America acknowledges her dependence on God, we could lose this freedom that's so dear to us.

Prayer has changed the course of history in the past. It is still as powerful today. "If my people, which are called by my name, shall humble themselves, and pray, and seek my face, and turn from their wicked ways. Then will I hear from heaven, and will forgive their sin, and will heal their land."

The late President Kennedy, in his inaugural address, said, "Do not ask what your country can do for you, but ask what you can do for your country." Pray, pray that our United States of American may continue as a nation under God.

In any election year, I beseech you to thoroughly understand what the candidate's platforms are. Seek the truth, do not be misled. Ask questions. Do they believe in God? Will they stand up for America during items of tribulation? Are their beliefs and yours cohesive? These are the people that will represent you. Are they truly your choice?

Take time out of your busy schedule and study the issues, know your candidates. Most of all, get out and vote when the time comes. Too many Americans suffer from apathy. They refuse to take responsibility for what has happened to our country. It's our fault. Yours and mine. It's our country, yours and mine. It's time that we face the problems instead of ignoring them. They will not go away. They are only becoming worse.

Why did we vote to take prayer out of the schools? Were we afraid that it would poison our children, or did it come about because we suffered from apathy and just did not respond? This is one small example of what can happen if we are sleeping. Our country will not be taken over from outside but from within. Failure to recognize the insidious workings of a different doctrine will allow it to grow and spread and become acceptable, even fashionable.

Why should publicly lighted crosses be forced to be taken down because a few people find it disagreeable? Why should the nativity scenes be taken from city and government property at Christmas time because it offends someone? This is a free country, and each of us has the right to self-expression. When we take away these rights, we are limiting our power.

Today the greatest need of our country is prayer. It is also the greatest need of national and world leaders today. As we recognize the seriousness of these times, we need to turn to God in intercessory prayer.

How often have the past events of history been changed because of prayer? Prayer is of primary importance. We are reminded to pray for all men everywhere. I have read that if we pray for one country each day, we will pray for the entire world three times in one year. To us, the Christian God has given us the privilege of praying. Our country desperately needs our intercession these days. May we join hearts in prayer for our beloved United States of America and for her people no matter where they are, what they are, or who they are?

May God Bless America.

FAITH

Man has struggled for four thousand years to coat himself with the veneer of civilizations. He has worked himself up from the caves to communities, from selfishness to social consciousness, from grunts to refined articulation. He has taught himself many things, but he still does not always have faith.

Faith is the most important of all human gifts. Without it, the world becomes unhinged. How long would a marriage last without faith? Think about that, how long would a marriage last without faith. Man has split an atom yet has never seen it. How did he know positively that it was there? Millions of people in the world believe in God, but how certain are they that there is no hereafter. The Old Testament and the New are full of references to the promises of God to man; if one believes in him, how can it be doubted that he will not welcome the children of faith to his kingdom. The good Father is always portrayed as understanding and forgiving.

Proof is another matter. It not only eliminates the primary need for faith, but it would, in time, alter the fruitfulness of man by making him seek death and the hereafter—eternity—

instead of continuing a struggle for bread and life. What would be the point of working on this land of ours if we had proof that blissful life everlasting was assured. However, with all the faith at our command, we are left with an instinct to live on and on. We try to stay here because we fear the unknown. If we knew for sure, it would be different. It is unnecessary to be a divine or chosen one to understand God and what He expects of us and what he has promised.

Faith is the most easily and often berated of all the virtues. I could read the Bible to you, and you could tell me that it is phony, and I cannot prove that you are wrong. Faith implies an absence of truth.

You have it, or you do not; if you do not, then you have cancer of the soul. You have erosion of the soul; you have doubt ... and that doubt will continue to increase, and you will end up believing in nothing. Not even yourself.

However, God is becoming more and more popular in the United States; more than one hundred million people go to services. Think about that, more than one hundred million people go to services, and that's not counting those that do not attend services but believe in God. That's a tremendous amount of faith being demonstrated. Of course, some go through the love of God, some through fear, and a few because it's fashionable.

To my way of thinking, this mass procession of faith imposes an increasing burden on the clerics, the ministers, rabbis, and priests. They have the people with them, but the job is to hold them ... and piety alone will not do it. It is not enough for a preacher to sit up in the late hours of the night writing the outline of a sermon. He must be a bridge between God and man or woman. Where many preachers fail, I believe, is where they imply by attitude and by direction that they alone only have the personal endorsement of God and that all others do not. The more they emphasize the wrath of God, the less they discuss God's love for all men, women, and children. The more they call for justice, the less they know about mercy. No sinner wants justice; instead, they cry out for compassion. I have never met an atheist who was insincere. The atheist has a sightless soul ... because he has not seen God, he refuses to believe. Yet if he would only have faith, the miracle of God would be revealed to him in many, many ways. There's that key word again ... faith.

There is a desperate need today for religious leaders to come closer to the people; ministers must become the bridge between the everyday world of small triumphs and huge heartaches that face us all. They must become the bridge to God. The leaders of each congregation have never had a better opportunity than they have right now ... as people approach God through the ministers, so might the ministers get closer to God through the people. A minister can best help by teaching those in search of faith to simply believe, helping still others to restore their faith, and helping us all perpetuate our faith, our belief in our Father.

I have heard people cry out, "I have faith ... I believe ... I pray ... yet nothing happens." First, you must believe in the power of prayer. You must know how to pray correctly; really, it's very simple. You must be alone and speak out loud. Say your prayer to God or Jesus so that he can hear. Talk out loud. Talk to him as you would a cherished friend or a loved one, and be assured that he will answer. You may not hear him immediately, but the answer will be there very clearly for you in the next few days. A yes answer is always quite clear. A no answer also is usually obvious. Often, we do not wish to accept it and try desperately to reject it, but the answer is obvious. The most difficult answer to accept is wait. It is the hardest to understand. When people cry out, "I have not received an answer." Their answer is clearly wait; you must have patience. Wait a week, a month, a year, five years, or maybe even twenty. In reality, it does not really matter, for when you look back, it's nothing but a wink of the eye of a star in the universe.

So, what is faith? Faith is an undying, all-believing love of our Lord Jesus and Father God. Faith comes from within, the belief that you are one with your Father, a serenity, a peace, a contentment with life. As stated in Hebrews, Book II, Chapter 1, "Faith is the substance of things hoped for, the evidence of things not seen."

I would like to share with you a thought that has been handed down in my family for several generations ... Today, tomorrow, and in the weeks and months ahead, keep this in your heart and remember ... Dreams long dwelt on amount to prayers, and prayers wrought in faith come true.

EVANGELIST WHITEFIELD

Through all ages, God has answered the needs of many by finding within the ranks of men themselves the great leaders who spread his word and who become a rock for the people of that era to rally around. Such a man was George Whitefield. Considered the greatest evangelist of the eighteenth century. He is one of the handful of men in the history of Christendom to be used by God to change the course of nations through the power of the Holy Spirit.

It was in the year 1733 that an eager English lad of 19 named George Whitefield went to Oxford to begin his first year of advanced education. From the start, young George was determinedly devout. He first tried to win God's approval by bringing his word to people in prisons and the poor houses. He joined John Wesley's famous "Holy Club" that put great emphasis on a disciplined spiritual life.

All of these things failed to fulfill young Whitefield until he read a book titled *The Life of God in the Soul of Man*. It was then that he read that all the good things he had been doing to earn God's favor were of no account. What he needed, he learned, was to have Christ formed within him; in short, he needed to be born again.

This discovery was the turning point for this talented young man. He was ordained at the age of twenty-two, and from the first, his great preaching set off a series of revivals.

The so-called "Boy Preacher" felt his true calling was in the New World, and it was first in Georgia that his mighty words captured the hearts and minds of the hearers.

We have seen what vast crowds Billy Graham's crusades can draw and the real conversions of so many thousands of Americans in the major cities in which they are held. We have seen thousands come to see and hear the late Kathryn Kuhlman, and we have all read of the great numbers who convened for Billy Sunday and of entire towns converted on a single night in the preaching and healing ministry of Dr. Alfred Price. Even so, the impact George Whitefield had on America was something we may never see again.

Like lightning, using God to tie it all together, he fanned the embers of revival up and down the eastern seaboard. Even Benjamin Franklin, the confirmed agnostic, became his fast friend and wrote glowing reports of Whitefield's work, giving generous contributions to his cause.

It was nothing for Whitefield to preach a hundred times in six weeks, sometimes even as much as four times a day. This ever-pressing schedule caused him to pay a fearful toll in health, but he would tell everyone that in being born again, his life belonged to Christ, and doing God's work was his only reason for being on this Earth.

Between 1736 and 1770, Whitefield preached more than eighteen thousand sermons. In his preaching, people began to discover a fundamental truth which would be a major foundation stone of God's new nation, and which by 1776 would be declared self-evident: "that in the eyes of their creator, all men were of equal value."

In 1770 Whitefield's health was broken and his breathing tormented by asthma attacks, yet he drove himself as never before. Although his voice was just a whisper, he asked God for strength for one last sermon, and God answered his prayers. For two hours, in a clear, resonant voice and blessed with inner fire, George Whitefield spoke to his new New Hampshire audience.

George Whitefield died the following morning as the first rays of the sun came through his window. He died knowing that his dream had come true. American was a nation now —"One Nation Under God."

EASTER SEASON

The Easter season now unfolds and it's springtime once again.
The countryside has come alive throughout the entire glen.
The meadows glow in emerald green as they stretch along the way
And flowers bloom just everywhere in colors bright and gay.

The lovely birds all hop about and sing their happy songs;
This masterpiece that Nature's made to everyone belongs.
Just everything that Nature grows upon this very earth,
At Easter time she tells to all. The story of rebirth.

GOOD FRIDAY

Today is recognized by Christians around the world as Good Friday. Millions will commemorate the momentous event that occurred almost 2,000 years ago, the crucifixion of the Lord Jesus on the cross of Calvary.

Some students of the Bible think it occurred on Thursday, while others are convinced it happened on Wednesday. My purpose here is not to discuss whether it should be Good Wednesday, Good Thursday, or Good Friday. As important as that subject may be, I simply want to remind you of the profound significance of the grand event.

The origin of this observance is unknown and why the name Good Friday was used is also uncertain. In early times, it was referred to as long Friday. Probably because of the length of the services held on that day. Some authorities say that originally it was called God's Friday. Soon we'll be celebrating Christ's resurrection, but today let us pause to thank the heavenly father for his gift of love and for the real meaning of the Savior's sacrifice on the cross at Calvary.

It was no mere martyr's death. It was not just a great show of deed.
It was not simply a miscarriage of justice.
Rather, when the Lord Jesus hung between earth and sky,
Shedding his blood and giving his life,
He was paying for the sins of the entire world.
As a result, salvation, forgiveness, and everlasting life
can be enjoyed by anyone who places his trust in him.
And all of this possible because of the Fathers love for us.
No wonder some call it God's Friday.
Know as life grows older, and our eyes have clearer sight
that under each wrong, somewhere there lives the root of right
That each sorrow has its purpose, by the sorrowing often unseen,
But as sure as the sun brings morning, whatever is, is best
He knows that each sinful action as sure as the night brings shade,
Is somewhere sometime punished, through the hour be long delayed.
We know that the soul is aided sometimes by the hearts unrest, and to
grow, means often to suffer.
But whatever is, is best.
We know there are no errors, in the great eternal plan, and all things
work together for the final good of man.
And we know as our soul speeds upward,
In its grand eternal quest,
We shall say, as we look back earthward,
Whatever is, is best.

GOOD FRIDAY AND EASTER

Turn your thoughts back to the time of Christ's life upon this Earth. It is Friday and the long hours of unbearable suffering come to an end as he gives his spirit to his father.

Now it is over, and the torn and tortured body is removed from the cross, bathed, dressed, and taken to the tomb.

This now is the end of life, the end of all struggles, happiness, hopes, and fears, the end ... the final chapter ... nothing more.

Feel the cold of the tomb as it penetrates every fiber. Now the stone is rolled over the mouth of the tomb, and eternal darkness and increasing cold surround us.

Silence ... pitch-black silence ... the dampness and the cold ... death has won the victory... this is the end of life forever. Just the cold .... the darkness ... then from

far, far away, a pinpoint, a gleam ... a glimmer of light.

From as far away as eternity itself we hear his voice .... I made a promise ... a promise of everlasting life ... believe and follow my voice.

Into the depth of the tomb comes the first soft breath of

perfumed warm air. Slowly, ever so slowly, we rise and move toward the pinpoint of light, and as we move forward, the light increases and the warmth surrounds us, and the icy dampness leaves our body, and we feel young and strong again. In the blaze of all the light of heaven, we step through the mouth of the tomb, and as far as the eye can see are fields of lilies ... gently moving in the soft summer air, lilies white, and blossoms atop long green stems. Lilies, pure and beautiful, are the symbol of God's love and God's promise to us of everlasting life.

Death has no victory, God has kept his promise of life after death, and in the beauty of the lilies, we find his eternal love of his glory this Easter morning.

EASTER

To all crying saints, dry every tear.
For your departed Lord, Behold the place - he is not here.
The tomb is all unbarred ... the gates of death were closed in Vain.
the Lord is Raised, He lives again.

Now cheerful to the house of prayer ... your early footsteps bend.
The Savior will himself be there ... our advocate and friend.
Once by the law your hopes were slain. But now in Christ you live again.
Now tranquil, now the rising day ... for Jesus still appears

A risen Lord, to chase away your unbelieving fears.
Weep no more, the Lord is raised, he lives again.

COMMUNION SUNDAY

Today, this morning, we step out in new faith and with new enthusiasm to meet the good that this day holds. I bless the past and release it into the timelessness of infinity. For today, this morning, is the time to step out in new faith. There are no limitations on this faith. It is boundless and limitless. We meet and make new opportunities, opportunities which yesterday our imagination could not picture, our eyes could not see, our hands could not hold. Now is the time for new happiness. If yesterday left anything to be desired, today finds new avenues of happiness opening in each of us. There will be happiness in our hearts, in our homes, and in every place we go. It will be a happiness that is shared, a never-ending happiness.

Today is new, and you are a new person, for God has filled each of us with a new faith and new enthusiasm, and we welcome new opportunities for new happiness. It is our joy to step out in faith to meet the good that this day holds.

As we hear the words from Corinthians, Chapter 2. Verse 5, "Therefore, if anyone is in Christ, he is a new creation. The old has passed away. Behold, the new has come."

Nothing can limit us, bind us, or defeat us. For we are free with the freedom of the Holy Spirit.

Praise the Lord for your life is now with him, unlimited life, pure and perfect. Now sit quietly and praise him over and over and receive your special message or healing.

You are now at peace with yourself.

You are calm in body and mind.

You're master now of your entire being

You realize you must do this in order to bring into expression your spiritual senses.

You must be calm and serene in order to acquire the habit of attention

You are in a complete state of realization.

You are giving attention now to your progress in spiritual enfoldment.

You're mastering the art of mediation.

You are God expressed.

You are at peace.

We search for God in churches.

We search for God in books.

We search for God in miracles divine.

But when we learn that God is found in every place there is.

The joy of finding God is truly ours.

SUMMER

A DESERT PLACE

I would like to remind you of the words of our Lord, "He said to them, come aside into a desert place, and rest a while," Luke, Chapter 9.

Today we will take a trip out into the desert that is to be found in Southern California near the Arizona Border. You have just parked your car, and you step out to walk into the desert. Now, find a nice quiet place and sit in quiet contemplation.

The Lord's early ministry was marked by frequent periods of prayer and silent communion with the Father.

When his disciples were weary from their evangelistic tours, and the pressure of the crowd was beginning to tell on them, physically, the Savior would take them into a quiet place to rest. We, too, must regularly lay aside our work and spend some time in meditation before the Lord. This kind of needed retreat is like an oasis in the desert where the body can rest, and the spirit can revive for coming emergencies and additional service.

The great prophet Elijah exhausted himself in the work of

the Lord and ended up famished and despondent under a juniper tree. If Jesus's disciples and that mighty prophet needed quiet periods to recuperate and to nourish the inner man, certainly we require the same in these days of added pressures. We need time to nourish the inner man or inner woman. Physical fatigue and spiritual floundering often go hand in hand. Every believer requires time out in the rapid and rugged game of life to relax his body and refresh his soul. Bless oh Lord these quiet times with thee, when heart and mind are still, and let our meditation be, according to thy will.

Sit now quietly in silence for a few minutes and communicate with God.

It is now time that we return this morning from the desert. Slowly get up from your quiet place in the desert, pick up your belongings, and start your walk back to your car. As you look around, the ground seems more alive with tiny objects, the sky seems bluer, the air fresher, and as you walk, you feel terrific. Your body is stronger and more alive than it has been for a long time.

You have just experienced a spiritual time-out. You are now better prepared to face the world around you. As you reach your car and begin your drive back to town, you realize why it is so very important to take time out to rejuvenate your body and mind. Make a promise to yourself to try and find a few moments each day to reach this peaceful state.

RAINDROPS

As we climb up our heavenly stairway, we begin to enter into a beautiful, lush garden spot, and standing in the middle of this plush garden with green ferns, roses, and plants of all types stands our teacher Jesus. He stands in a brilliant shaft of light; gold and white light surround him. He beckons to us to join him. We approach him timidly and a little in awe. He tells us to sit at his feet, for he has a message for us. As we settle ourselves comfortably at his feet, we notice a slight rain begins to fall all around us. However, we are now inside the shaft of white light, and here it is dry and safe. Yet just outside the light, the rain continues to fall. Our Lord Jesus tells us today his message is regarding the legend of the raindrop. And now we understand why it is raining.

The raindrop has a lesson for us all.
    As it trembles in the heavens questioning whether it should fall
        for the glistening raindrop argued to the teacher in the sky,

I am beautiful and lovely as I sparkle here on high,
and hanging here I will become part of the rainbow's hue
and I'll shimmer like a diamond for the entire world to view.

But the teacher told the raindrop do not hesitate to go
for you will be more beautiful if you fall to the earth below.

For you will sink into the soil and be lost a while from sight,
but when you reappear on earth, you'll be looked on with delight,

for you will be the raindrop that quenches the thirsty ground
and helped the lovely flowers to blossom all around.

And in your resurrection, you'll appear in queenly clothes
with the beauty of the lily and the fragrance of the rose.

Then when you wilt and wither, you'll become part of the earth
and make the soil more fertile and give new flowers birth.

For there is nothing ever lost or eternally neglected
for everything God ever named is always resurrected.

So, trust God's all wise wisdom and doubt the Father never,
for in his heavenly kingdom there is nothing lost forever.

Our teacher tells us it is time to go but asks that we remember these few lines of the legend of the raindrop whenever trouble overtakes us, and we feel lost in dark clouds. It is now time to slowly walk downward on our lovely star-studded stairway.

GARDEN TEACHER

Today we will take a walk on a heavenly stairway. As we ascend the first step, we take a deep breath and hold it slightly until we become light-headed. Then we let the breath go and relax, letting the cares of this week slip away. And so on to the second, third, and fourth steps, we repeat this process. Letting our bodies completely relax. We climb higher, higher, and higher until we enter a lush garden spot. Standing in the middle of the garden is our teacher, Jesus. Many words and thoughts began to take place in your mind, and the words rush forward into your throat, and you hear yourself saying:

"I could not leave thee, Christ, for when I tried to leave you for alluring ways aside from thine own way, thy power withheld me, kept my feet from wandering too far, inept and aimless, down a dwindling path that led through mazed confusion to the house of dread.

I could not leave thee, Christ, for when I yearned with passionate intensity and burned with fiery torment to quench my thirst for freedom by a turbulent stream that burst in gushing torrents from a naked hill, thee lead me back to waters deep and still.

I could not leave thee, Christ, for when I sought to fling aside your counsel when I thought that in my crazy freedom I should find some way of life for body, soul, and mind better than thou did teach, I heard you say come back to me, child, for you have lost your way.

I would not enslave thee, Christ, for I am lame from wandering, and the consuming flame of passion has gone out and left my soul a smoldering ember, and the crisscrossed scroll of life ends as it started with the line, I cannot leave thee, Christ, for I am thine

MEDITATION

Are you very weary? Rest a little bit.
Seek some quiet corner, fold your hands and sit.
Do not let the worries that have grieved you all the day
haunt this quiet corner. Drive them all away.
Let your heart grow empty of every thought unkind.
That peace may hover over you. And joy may fill your
　　mind.
Soon you'll feel so rested, so glad you stopped a bit
in this quiet corner, to fold your hands and sit.

REDECORATE YOUR MIND

From Romans Chapter 12, Verse 2, "And be not conformed to this world, but be ye transformed by the renewing of our mind, that ye may prove what is that good, and acceptable, and perfect will of God.

The mind of man is some part of the mind of God; therefore, it contains within itself unlimited possibilities of expansion and self-expression.

If you wanted to renew a room in your house, you might take down the old pictures and curtains. Move out the drab and worn-out furniture and clean out all of the accumulated cobwebs and dust. You would vacuum the floors and give the walls a fresh coat of paint. You would wash the windows to let in the sunshine. Next, you would begin to furnish your room with the bright, colorful things that were pleasing to you. You would choose comfortable furniture and cheerful pictures. You would make your room a happy, pleasant place to be.

You can renew your mind in just the same way that you renew a room in your house. Take down the old pictures of fear and failure. Move out all the drab and worn-out ideas. Clean the windows of your mind to let in the light in. Then begin to bring in things that please you. It is your very own private room, and you deserve the very best furniture and the most beautiful pictures in your mind.

Think that your mind is part of the mind of God. Begin today to clean out the thoughts of lack and limitation which have kept you from expressing this perfect mind of God in your life. Let the light come in.

The truth is that each of you has the unlimited potential to express your best self every day. The room of your mind can be clean and bright and cheery, proving the good and perfect will of God in your life, constantly renewing and expanding your understanding of the limitless possibilities within yourselves.

Your mind is a storeroom. A mini-computer that functions with the information that you feed it. If we program our minds with thoughts of God. with thoughts of joy, with thoughts of helpfulness to others, we will reach a little closer to join our mind with the divine mind of God.

Today, I would like you to think about redecorating your mind. Fill it fully. Furnish it with thoughts and information that will take you one step closer, one step higher, to that divine wisdom that has been delivered to a few great prophets. Perhaps you do not wish to be a prophet. Then realize that by clearing your mind and redecorating with healthier spiritual thoughts, you will become a better person. Thoughts take action, and your life will change. Try it and see the improvement, or at the very least, be a project under construction, working each day toward a healthier spiritual being.

MIRACLE

What will you do with your miracle?

Wherever you live, whether you saw it or not, you were given a miracle to start this day. God put a sunrise in the sky, just for you.

Each sunrise happens only once. No two look exactly alike. No sunrise remains long in any one place.

I've seen many, many sunrises, and each time I've watched the eastern sky lighten to an azure blue frame for the sun, I've felt new gratitude for the heavenly father who begins each of our days with this miracle of beauty, power, and light. With this, as with every other miracle, we must use it or lose it.

Perhaps as you hear these words, God is sending another and very personal sunrise into your heart. It's the bright dawning of another miracle. The realization that the spirit is calling you to a larger partnership in worldwide faith and ministries of renewal and reconciliation in Christ. What will you do with this miracle of today? God's gift of this day and his unique invitation to serve him joyfully with all you have and are. Only you can give the answer.

Reach back in your memory and find a sunrise that seems the most outstanding. Now concentrate on that sunrise and also concentrate on God's plan for you. What can you do today to help develop yourself?

COMMISSIONED BY CHRIST

Is it enough for us to believe in God and to try to lead a moral life? No, not really.

All of us are commissioned by Christ to go out and tell others of God's mercy and love and to try to bring them into God's family. This is not only a duty commanded by Christ but a privilege which we should rejoice to do in thanksgiving and love. Since we ourselves have received God's revelation and the Christian faith through others, we ought to show our thanks by being the means by which others may come to know God and to believe in him. If we love our neighbors as Christ commanded us, we cannot help but share this most precious gift with them.

What do we call this sharing, and how is it done?

It is called evangelism, spreading the good news, and it is done by word and by the witness of our lives. We should tell others what we have learned and experienced and what God has done for us through Christ. Reading Christian books may help us to express this in words, and we can introduce these books, as well as the Bible, to those outside the family of

Christianity. Our lives are also a most important witness. When we show God's love and Christian joy in our lives, others will see, and this will help to lead them to Christ. It is through that, because we have different gifts, some can lead others more easily. But all of us can do something. Bring someone to Christ. Lend a Christian book or make a witness in our lives.

We frequently hear the term born again. What does it mean? What is a born-again Christian? When you speak of born again, you speak of joining the family of God and that you receive Christ as his son and your savior, and God the Holy Spirit as the one who lights the candle of faith within.

Having a born-again experience means that you are reaffirming the religious foundation of your younger years. People without any religious training whatsoever also experience a sudden religious feeling and sometimes refer to this as being born again. A changing of their lifestyles and a seeking to follow in the Lord's path. I once heard an elderly minister answer the question, "How do you become born again?" He asked the young lady, "Do you believe in Jesus Christ as your Lord and savior." She answered, "Yes." "Do you believe in the teachings of the Bible?" Are you ready to live your life in the teachings of the Bible?" "Are you ready to live your life by it?" She answered, "Yes." The last question he asked was, "Are you ready to do it now?" She answered, "Yes." At that point, he asked God to reach out and touch this young woman's life. I know that it works because that young woman was me. You, too, can be born again. Simply ask yourself the questions I asked. "Do you believe in Jesus Christ as your savior, the son of God?" "Do you believe in the teachings of the Bible, and are you ready to live your life by it" "Are you ready to do it now?" If you answered yes to all the questions, then ask God to reach out and touch you and bless you. Be assured that he will. Know that he will.

Once you're born again, remember that you have the power to help someone else to come to the Lord. Do not be afraid to witness before someone or reach out a helping hand, for sometimes, one kind word can change the destiny of an individual's life from one of self-destruction to a life of joy and hope and spiritual fulfillment. I know, for it changed mine.

RAPHAEL

Arch-Angel Raphael ("God has healed") of Chaldean origin, originally called Labial. Raphael is one of the three great Archangels in post-biblical lore. He first appears in the Book of Tobit (a work external to the Hebrew canon, apocryphal in Protestant Scripture, canonical in Catholic). In the Book of Tobit, Raphael acts as a companion and guide to Tobit's son Tobias who journeys to Media from Nineveh. It is only at the end of the journey that Raphael reveals himself by name as "one of the seven holy angels" that attend the Throne of God.

Raphael is charged to heal the Earth, and through him, the Earth furnishes an abode for man, whom he also heals of his maladies.

Raphael is one of the three angels that visited Abraham (Genesis 18)—the other two angels identified are usually Gabriel and Michael.

Raphael is credited with healing Abraham of the pain of circumcision, the patriarch neglecting to observe this rite earlier in life.

In the Legend of the Jews, Raphael is the angel sent by God

to cure Jacob of the injury to the thigh when Jacob wrestled with his dark adversary at Penile.

Another legend claims it was Raphael who handed Noah, after the flood, a "medical book," which may have been the famous "Sefer Raziel" (The Book of the Angel Raziel).

Among other high offices, Raphael is the regent of the sun, chief of the order of virtues, governor of the south, guardian of the west, ruling prince of the 2nd heaven, overseer of the evening winds, guardian of the Tree of Life in the Garden of Eden, one of the six angels of repentance, and the angel of prayer, love, joy, and light. Above all, he is, as his name denotes, "the Angel of Healing."

JOY

Webster's dictionary states "joy" is a glad feeling—happiness, delight. The Bible mentions the word joy forty-five times, and the word joyful is used fifteen times. Joy stands for Jesus, Others, and You.

If you place Jesus first in your life, everything else will fall into place perfectly. Then place others, your family, your loved ones, and your friends next. Stop and consider how your actions will affect these people. Are you doing something that will hurt them? Perhaps a kind word or gesture could really make a difference in their lives. All too often, we only consider ourselves in a selfish, vain way and never stop to realize that if we made a special effort to extend ourselves to others, they would return this kindness. Our lives would be enriched by the actions bringing joy back to you.

Jesus, Others, and You.

The Bible makes it quite clear that the joy of the Lord is our strength. In Nehemiah, Chapter 8, we find Ezra, the priest and scribe, bringing the book of the Law of Moses, which the

Lord had commanded to Israel. You should read this if at all possible. It elaborates on the use of the word "Joy." In that quote, it is made quite clear that the "Joy of the Lord is our strength in all that we do."

BLESSED ARE THE MEEK

Blessed are the meek, for they shall inherit the Earth. Doesn't that sound ridiculous? We live in a high-powered, dynamic, energetic promotional country called the United States of America. Don't we all know that it is the high-energy, powerful promoter and big wheeler-dealer that gets ahead? Blessed are the meek, for they shall inherit the Earth. If Jesus had said, "Blessed are the meek, for the IRS is the kingdom of heaven." That we could understand. But when he said, "Blessed are the meek, for they shall inherit the Earth," it sounds like a gross statement of ridicule. Until you study the Greek origin of the word "bless," you cannot really understand what the word means. I will not give you a lesson in Greek, but I did translate that saying in several other ways to clarify the meaning.

Blessed are the patient. They shall overcome their problems and work through their difficulties. They shall preserve their family and friends. They shall gain ground, acquire an education, have money, build lasting relationships, lay solid foundations, and will truly succeed in the blessings of living life on this earth. Blessed are the patient. They shall inherit the earth's highest achievements.

Blessed are the emotionally controlled. They shall hold their tongues. They shall tame their wild tempers. They shall develop a disciplined divine poise. They shall hold in check their negative impulses. They shall avoid and resist distractions and temptations which would excite and stimulate. But drain their financial, moral, and physical resources. Blessed are the emotionally controlled. They will make successes of their lives on this Earth.

Blessed are the honest. Hard-working folks, they are more interested in substance than popularity ratings. They are more dedicated to making solid achievements than to making fast but phony happiness. They are quick to pass on the credit to others. Blessed are they, for they shall be loved and respected by good people in this life.

Blessed are the teachable, for they shall learn much before it is too late. Blessed are those who know what it is that they do not know and are eager to listen to older, wiser, and more experienced seers. Blessed indeed are they who, in true meekness, remember that a little learning is a dangerous thing. Blessed are those who never forget that they are never too old to learn. Blessed are they, for they shall inherit great wisdom and, with it, success.

Blessed are the sensitive spirits. They shall inherit the affection of all good people. Happy indeed is the heart which is sensitive to another's insecurity. Loving is he who offers reassurance to another's hostility, affection to another's loneliness, friendship to another's hurt, and apologies to all. Blessed are such sensitive souls, for they shall inherit the devotion and esteem of good people on this earth.

Blessed are the powerful people. They have learned to restrain their power. They know that the real power is in its control and discipline, lest it rips out the tender plants of human kindness and gentleness. Yes, blessed are those who remain gentle while they build strength, who are merciful while they are mighty, blessed are they, for they shall not merely win a war, they shall win the hearts of a nation.

Blessed are the quiet people who do so much good for so many without fanfare, glory-seeking, or headline hunting. They shall inherit the trust, respect, and love of the truly beautiful people on this Earth.

Blessed are the truly creative persons. They turn their problems into projects. Their sorrows into servants. Their difficulties into dividends, their obstacles into opportunities, their tragedies into triumphs, and their stumbling blocks into stepping stones. They look upon an interruption as an interesting interlude. They harvest fruit from frustration. They convert enemies into friends. They look upon adversities as adventures. Blessed are they, for they shall inherit self-respect in their life.

Blessed are the truly humble. They shall seek truth, knowing they lost it. They shall surely find it. They shall accept criticism, knowing that they are not perfect. They shall yield the floor to those who are better informed. They shall be big enough to say, "I'm sorry, and I am wrong." Happy are the humble hearted for, they shall receive forgiveness from their God and their fellow man. They shall receive peace of mind on this Earth.

Blessed are those who are willing to be third. Happy are those who put Jesus first, others second, and themselves third in line. Richly rewarded in this life are those who learn the lesson of our Lord "that if any man would be a master, let him also be a servant. If anyone would be first, he must be first of all a servant of all." For whosoever would save his life will lose it, and whosoever loses his life for my sake, he will save it.

Blessed are they, for they shall inherit a beautiful life on this Earth.

Blessed are the God-shaped Christ molded people—Bishop Fulton Sheen once said, "Some come in chariots, some on horses, but we come in the name of the Lord." Yes, blessed are those humble people who come, not with a big splash and lot of show, but who honestly come carrying the word of the Lord.

It begins to make sense, doesn't it? Blessed are the meek, for they shall inherit the Earth.

Of course, consider if, by contrast, cursed is the cocky, arrogant, haughty, boastful underdog, for he will have few friends. Unhappy is the elbowing, crowding, shoving, pushing, get-out-of-my-way-I'm-first bully, for he shall make many enemies. I want to do it my way, deaf to constructive criticism, careless of shrewd counsel, and indifferent to warnings, he is headed for a fall. Doomed is the hothead. Pride and uncontrolled temper come before the fall. Unhappy is the man who loses his cool and is too proud to say, "I'm sorry." He will never inherit the Earth. He will not ever hold his job, or perhaps his wife. Hell-bent on this Earth are the impatient, restless, rootless, and ruthless promoters. They may gain a crow and lose the kingdom. What shall it profit a man if he gains the world and loses his own soul?

Blessed are the meek, for they shall inherit the Earth begins to sound like the best advice ever offered for happy living. Indeed, it is true. In the long pull, those who win the world around them are those who Jesus calls the meek, the controlled, the patient, the honest, the quiet, the forceful, the powerful but restrained, disciplined, and poised person. He is God molded, Christ shaped, spirit dominated.

Blessed are the meek, for they shall inherit the Earth. Love on this Earth shall inherit the Earth.

Blessed are the meek, for they shall inherit the Earth. Jesus provided it. Above all, he was led like a lamb to the slaughter. Despised, rejected by men. A man of sorrow who was acquainted with grief, Pontius Pilate thought he had won. Herod was sure that Jesus had lost. Everybody was convinced this fellow was wiped out for good. Today, who is alive? Jesus Christ is alive. Pilate is dead. Blessed are the meek, for they shall inherit the Earth. Give God time, and it will always work our way.

Now, look at the ultimate example of the truly meek. Look at Jesus Christ. He was controlled emotionally, spat upon, insulted, stripped, ridiculed, and despised. He was led as a lamb to the slaughter. Yet, he never struck back. Foolish? He inherited the Earth, didn't he? There's not a land where Jesus is not loved.

He demonstrated quiet determination steadfastly; he set his face to Jerusalem. He knew what he had to do. He did it. A sacrifice on the cross. Ridiculous? Insane? He inherited the Earth, didn't he? Men of every color and motivation kneel before him.

He was gentle, kind, forgiving, loving, even to those who killed him. Stupid, you say? Was it? He could face God with a clear conscience when he died. It is finished, he said. Today the world loves him. His enemies. They are truly dead. Pilate, who used power without love, lives on in infamy. Suffered under Pontius Pilate is a phrase repeated by millions of churches in the apostles' creed. But Christ lives on.

I remember the lines of a great poet who said:

I saw the conquerors riding by with cruel lip and faces wan,

Musing on empires, sacked and burned,

There rode the Mongol Genghis Khan and Alexander, like a God

Who sought to weld the world in one and Caesar with his Laurel wreath

and a thing from hell - the Hun.
And Leading like a star the van
Heedless of up stretched arm and groan
Inscrutable Napoleon rode dreaming of empire and alone.

But they all perished from the scene like fleeting shadows on a glass

and conquering down the centuries comes Christ, the Sword less,

riding on an ass.

PENSIONERS ALL

I am a humble pensioner, myself, for my daily bread;
Shall I forget my brothers who seem in greater need?
I know not how it happened that I have more than they,
Unless God meant that I should give a larger part away.
The humblest wayside beggar and I have wants the same.
Close side by side we walked when God called out the name;
So brother, it happened the name he called was mine;
The food was given for both here, half of it is thine.

HOLISTIC HEALING

The true meaning of holistic healing—I prefer treatment as healing implies that you are ill. The term holistic treatment is something that can be used at times of sickness or otherwise to continue staying well.

Some people think the word means tribal rituals, crazy faith healers. It actually means "body, mind, and spirit as a whole." Oneness—physical, mental, and spiritual—working together all the time.

The ancient Chinese have stated that illness is the result of the individual being disharmonious with itself. We know that many illnesses are brought on by our state of mind, by emotional stresses and problems.

Touch healing is described as the laying on of hands in the Bible, which has been with us for many years. We know that it works in many cases. Think back when you have been ill. Having a family member sit with you or a close friend hold your hand is very comforting. Knowing someone cares eases the pain. Also, their energies are being sent to you this way, and that helps soothe the pain.

INSTEAD OF THERAPY

Touch healing is one of the most holistic approaches to getting well. Not a substitute for doctors or for prayer, but to be used in addition for extra help. So, if you suffer from an illness, whether physical or emotional, start today to program your mind for good health. The first step is to eliminate frustrations from your life, whether they are a child's frustrations with a parent, or vice versa, social pressures, sexual pressures, struggles for position or financial success, etc.

In time these frustrations, if not eliminated, will turn inward and cause sickness and ultimate disease. Eliminate them from your life today, forever.

Harmony with your life, with your body, and with your spiritual convictions are the keys to holistic healings or treatments. I believe we will hear a great deal more about this in the future.

Doctors today are finally saying they are not God. That they work with the will of God to help people. They are exploring new avenues of diet, mind concentration, and religious prayer to help patients that before they would have just given up on. Some open-minded doctors have expressed a willingness to try touch healing along with their tried-and-true medical procedures.

Reinforcing strength. Everyone is provided with the additional tool, the therapeutic tool of touching with hands. You can reach out and help someone.

Anyone near you can help by reaching out and sending you energy. A mother, father, husband, wife, son, or daughter can practice holistic healing in times of an emergency.

You receive healing from all the energies in the universe. If you have difficulty understanding how the healing energies work, put your hand in the air. You cannot see or feel radio or television signals, yet they are there passing through your hand to be received elsewhere. So, also are other communications like the healing energies. They pass through you, and often we do not even feel them. Some very attuned people, sensitives, will feel the healing energy as it passes through their bodies, using it as a battery or conductor, and on to another person.

All too often, we are told that religion and science are two separate worlds. Two separate fields. This really is not true, for when they are working together in a patient, the chance of a miraculous cure doubles its percentage.

One principle of sickness is that the body can make itself sick. Thus, it can also make itself well.

I feel that we are standing on the threshold of a new era, preventative medicine.

Preventative medicine might well mean holistic training for all. Learning to be in harmony with our minds, physical bodies, and spiritual capabilities.

Remember the steps:
Find the problem causing the illness.
Touch healing; laying on of hands, you can even use your own hands on your own body if necessary.
Eliminating frustrations and stresses in your life.
Program your mind that you will get well, that you will correct the physical problem.
Certainly, seek sound medical advice and remember, last but not least, that prayer is always heard by God.

These steps may save your life or the life of someone close to you.

FANNY CROSBY

Music has always been an essential part of Christian worship. Most of us, from the time we are little children, sing praises to God and through the years come to know and love many hymns. When I was just three years old, I first sang "Jesus Loves Me," and I have grown to love many great Christian hymns.

I wonder if you ever give a thought to the people who created these wonderful works of faith and beauty. There is a saying that great music is inspired by the angels, and maybe that's true.

Fanny Crosby was born in southeast New York State on March 24, 1820. This beautiful little girl became totally blind at the age of six weeks.

Despite this cruel handicap, Fanny, who later taught at the New York Institute for the Blind, had a wonderful and positive attitude toward life.

She would say, "Blindness cannot keep the sunlight of hope from the trusting soul. One of the earliest resolves that I formed in my young and joyous heart was to leave all care to yesterday and to believe that the morning would bring forth its own peculiar joy."

Truly wonderful words to live by.

In 1858 Fanny married Alexander Van Alstyne, who was also blind. Their united lives made harmony for forty-four years until his death in 1902. Alexander was a well-known church organist, and his cooperation and musical knowledge were key factors in Fanny's success.

And what success it was. Fanny Crosby wrote more than eight thousand religious poems. Many of which have become well-known hymns that have been distributed by the millions.

The list of titles includes "Jesus Keep Me Near The Cross," "Draw Me Nearer," "Blessed Assurance," "I Am Thine O'lord," and "All The Way My Savior leads Me."

Fanny Crosby's great hymn, "Safe in the Arms of Jesus," was one of the first American hymns to be translated into a variety of foreign languages.

It is almost unbelievable to realize that Fanny, although blind from the age of six weeks, produced nearly two hundred songs each year for forty years.

The next time you hear or sing, "Jesus Is Tenderly Calling Thee Home," "Savior More Than Life," or "Jesus Is Mine," please think of gentle Fanny Crosby, who knew that blindness could not keep the sunlight of hope from the trusting soul.

Fanny died in 1915 at the age of ninety-five after giving fifty-one years of her life to enriching Christian music.

If Fanny Crosby and her husband could accomplish so much in their lives and yet be totally blind, surely, we can close our eyes for a few moments of silent meditation and bring a small miracle into our own lives.

FLAW IN JESUS

The Christian scholars were worried; they had found a tiny flaw in the perfect life of Jesus.

It wasn't much of a flaw. It was comparable, perhaps to a baby gnat on the hide of an elephant, but perfection admits no error. Jesus the Messiah had condemned a fig tree for not bearing fruit. At that season, the tree wasn't supposed to have fruit.

The event occurred on the morning after Palm Sunday. Jesus and the twelve had spent the night at Bethany, three miles east of Jerusalem. Now, he was walking back to Jerusalem to teach on the temple steps in defiance of the high priests. That April morning was sun-spangled and cool.

Jesus walked ahead. The sun was behind him over the mountains of Moab. Much of the soil on the hills between the Mount of Olives and the Mount of Offense was gray and dead. The trees were few. Of these, a rare one was dressed in rich green leaves. The Messiah—tall, slender, a sad man who subjected himself to all the weakness and pain of men—saw the leafy tree. He was hungry. He approached the tree and stuck his hand in a branch and pulled outward. When he opened his palm, there was nothing but green leaves in it.

The apostles watched from a few feet off. Jesus pointed a finger at the tree and said, "May no man hereafter eat fruit of thee any more, forever." They passed on into Jerusalem, and that day Jesus cast out from the temple the money changers and overturned the tables and chairs of those who sold doves for sacrifice. The next morning, the apostles were passing the fig tree, and they noticed it had begun to wither.

Since that time, learned men have added bits and pieces to the life of Christ. One of the major discoveries was the date of his death. The scholars reasoned that the date of death was most likely April 6 in the year 30 AD. Assuming that this is true, then April 2 was the Monday on which he condemned the fig tree. In Palestine, figs are in good bloom in June.

This was the tiny flaw in the perfect life.

The theological riddle remained unsolved until the year 1880. At that time, an Oxford scholar named Alfred Edersheim was writing a big work entitled "The Life and Times of Jesus, The Messiah." When Edersheim came to the episode of the fig tree, he stopped work. He left England and went to Palestine so that he could examine a fig tree in early April. When he arrived, he sought the company of fellow scholars and Hebrew authorities, and like many others before and since, he traced all the holy places on foot.

In the first week of April, Mr. Edersheim found a fig in a leaf. He thrust his arm in, and when he pulled it out along the branch, he found that he had all gray substances in his hand. They looked like mushrooms.

"What are these?" he asked a Jewish professor. The man smiled. "Try them. They are good to eat. In the ancient days, travelers in the early spring ate them from trees while walking between towns."

Edersheim ate one. It tasted good. "Do you find them on all fig trees?" he asked.

"No," the professor said, "only on trees that will bear figs later. First, these in early spring, then figs. If a fig tree does not have these, it will have no figs in June."

The mystery had been solved. There was no flaw in the perfect life.

TO BE A FRIEND

The first step in the art of friendship is to be a friend. Then making friends takes care of itself.

To be a friend, one should start by being a friend to himself, by being true to his highest and best goals by aligning himself with the enduring values of human life that make for growth and strength.

To be a friend, one should strive to be like the shadow of a great rock in a weary land, to be a source of refuge and strength to those who walk alone.

To be a friend, one should believe in the inherent goodness of man and his potential greatness. We should treat people with a big spirit, expectant of a noble response.

To be a friend, one should strive to lift people up, not cast them down, to encourage, not discourage, and to set an example that will be an inspiration.

To be a friend, one should be sensitively responsive to the dreams and aims of others and show sincere appreciation for the contributions others make to the enrichment of one's own life.

To be a friend, one should practice the companionship of silence and the magic of words that your speech may build and not destroy, help and not hinder.

To be a friend, one should close his eyes to the faults of others and open them to his own.

To be a friend, one should not attempt to reform or reprimand but should strive only to make others as happy as possible.

To be a friend, one should be himself. He should be done with hypocrisy, artificiality, and pretense. He should meet and mingle with people in simplicity and humility.

To be a friend, one should be tolerant and have an understanding heart and forgiving nature, realizing that all people stumble now and then and that the person who never made a mistake never accomplished anything.

To be a friend, one should join hands with all who are working for great principles, great purpose, and great causes. He should put his shoulder to the wheel to work together to help achieve common goals.

To be a friend, one should go more than halfway in contact with others. Greet people first and not wait to be greeted. Radiate a spirit of overflowing goodwill.

To be a friend, one should remember that we are human magnets. That like attracts like, and that what we give, we receive.

To be a friend, one should recognize that the art of friendship is a lifetime study, that no person knows all the answers, and that we should add each day to our knowledge of how to live the friendly way. As we begin each new day, let us go out and make at least one new lasting friendship.

SPIRITUAL SIDE

People will ask, or will say, "You have a spiritual side, haven't you?"

Yes, sure I have. Less of a spiritual side than I would like to have, but it's there. It's real. No matter how many thousands of wrong things I've done, I've known that it was there. Every baby who draws the first gasping breath is equipped with a soul, a mind, and a body. As life proceeds, we tend to move from one to another of these three major pieces of equipment.

In the first twenty-five years, the body dominates. We love it. We adorn it. We hunger to please it.

In the second twenty-five years, we begin to lose faith in the body, and we turn toward the pleasures of the mind.

In the third twenty-five years, most of us remember we have a soul. The first two will betray you, not once but many times and in many ways. Only the soul remains constant and ageless.

When you have built-in faults as I have, it's fatal to be preachy. The teachers used to look through the front of my head and out the back, and they could read the crimes as though they had been written on a billboard. My one comfort used to come from thinking slowly of the commandments I hadn't broken.

When the soul dominates the mind and body, it is easy to see. My grandma had a bad Christmas before I was born. Three of her babies died, and instead of a tree, she had three white caskets in the living room. She looked at them dry-eyed. Then she dropped to her knees and said, "thy will be done" that was all.

Then there was Charlie Pearl. A Jew, Charlie owned a candy store. The morning that a Catholic orphanage burned down, Charlie shut the store, got into his car, and helped get the children out of the orphanage. Browbeat a restaurateur into donating twenty gallons of hot soup and went out to a farmer's market and came back with a load of vegetables. Charlie was in debt. He needed the pennies from the store.

There was Carry Porter. A Seventh Day Adventist. She was a plain woman who spent almost every moment of her life trying to do something for someone else. Anyone else. Her heart was so bad, some doctors were willing to listen to it for no fee just to make sure that it was still ticking. Cary Porter was kind even to those who tried to hurt her.

How, I ask myself, do you know you have a soul? I know just as sure as I know that I have a mind, and I have never seen that either. If I did see it, I wouldn't be able to tell you what makes it think.

YUCCA MOUNTAIN MANIA

The back history is all so hazy
Yet the state is going crazy
With Yucca Mountain madness
People are in all states of undress
Exposing their inner most feeling
Atomic blasts and nuclear war they are seeing
Running around attempting all sorts of actions
Trying desperately to untie all factions
The President says "It's a fate-a-compli"
Our Governor says "It will not be"
Our Mayor is raising community awareness
Most people are confused and under stress
What can we do to fight? This certainly is not right!
The answer of course, is we must unite
We must conquer our fears and frights
Perhaps there is a route that is realistic
Forget the egos and don't be materialistic
In the end, if we must accept this course

INSTEAD OF THERAPY

Let's sing Las Vegas praises until we are hoarse
For then all will know, it's too grand a city
To be brought down, we will accept no pity
We were originally created from dust
And we will rise again, if we must.

CANDELABRA

In all major religions of the world today, you will frequently see placed at the altar a candelabra holding seven candles, not the Jewish candelabra, which have nine candles. This is symbolic of the seven precepts of spiritualism. Commonly referred to as the Candles of Truth. Each candle is representative of one of the seven precepts. Anyone of the candles alone provides only a dim light, but the seven together furnish the necessary radiance for the vision and attainment of the ultimate in spiritual progression.

When fully lit, the candles illuminate with a mellow glow of peaceful understanding. Each of the seven precepts, which I will go into in just a moment, starts with the following letters: D, W, U, L, I, C, P. These letters can be translated into any easy way to remember what the meaning of the precepts stands for. Translated, they read, Divine Wisdom Utilizes Law in Cosmic Planning.

Spiritualism, as practiced in any religious faith, teaches that great religious truths are revealed to the mind of man by spirit teachers through inspiration and direct mediumship. The candelabra is the symbol of these teachings. Each candle represents each one of the seven precepts. The seven precepts are:

1. The first candle is Deity. The Lord is almighty God.

God is infinite, and being infinite encompasses within his being the activating principle of all life. All intelligence and all things. While a true and complete conception of God is impossible for our minds, nevertheless, we may know much about his attributes. Life, love, power, and intelligence.

2. Worship. Thou shall worship the Lord as God.

Man has a dual reaction to his environment—intellectual and emotional. His intelligence conceives the goodness and greatness of God. Producing an emotional reaction which is reverence. The worship of God and prayer open the mind and heart to higher spiritual knowledge and growth.

3. Universe. There is a natural world, and there is a spiritual world. The entire universe in both the seen and unseen phases is the manifestation of God. Man's knowledge of the universe in its natural phases is gained through the sciences and his five physical senses. His knowledge of the spiritual phases of the universe is gained through religion and his innermost spiritual faculties.

4. Law. Divine law is holy, and just and good.

Divine law, eternally inviolable and immutable, governs the universe and all its elements, one with another. The law of cause and effect, the natural laws of physics and chemistry, and the laws governing psychic and spiritual phases are all included in God's divine law, which maintains unity and order throughout the universe.

5. Immortality. The gift of God to all men is eternal life.

Man is a spirit inhabiting a physical body for a limited period. Whereupon that physical body is laid aside, and his existence continues in the spirit world. Death is but an incident in an endless life.

6. Communion. Man in the natural world and man in the spiritual world can communicate, one with the other.

Since mortals and spirits dwell in merely different phases of the one unified universe, communication between the two through mediumship is a natural process operating in accordance with divine law. Every mortal is a potential medium. Although certain individuals, because of natural gifts or talents, can develop mediumship to a more efficient degree than others.

7. Progression. All men shall turn to righteousness and dwell in the house of the Lord forever. From birth, man's spiritual development continues, perhaps retarded and retrograded, as he has complete freedom for moral choice, but deep within, there is a constant and instinctive urge for betterment. Every soul will progress through the ages to heights sublime and glorious. Death merely opens the gateway to a fuller and more radiant existence where the spirit of man develops and unfolds in the spirit spheres.

PAGES OF A BOOK

Life is a closed book that opens day by day. We live each of the pages.

Let's open our book to the beginning chapters. Chapters 1 to 12 resemble our early life from the years one to twelve. Were they happy? Would you change them? If so, change your chapters—re-write them to please you.

Now let's go on to Chapters 12 to 21. These are the bothersome years. Years of torture and self-doubt. Times of trial and tribulation. Also, years of learning, growing, and experiencing life.

The middle chapters are times of joy, happiness, marriage, children, career, success. If not, correct, change the paragraphs, delete the sentences you do not like.

As we begin to read the conclusion of our story, have we accomplished the entire plot of life? Have we told our story the way we would want others to write it down? How many chapters, paragraphs, sentences would we delete and rewrite differently? Would we phrase our life in a smoother flow of words and experiences, feelings and expressions?

And as we close the last page of the book and fold it together, is the story one we would recommend to a friend to read and follow the advice. Would you start at the very beginning and redo all the pages? How would you rate this book? Was it exciting? Pleasant? Enjoyable, good or sad, blue, void of feeling? Think about that, for you are rating your life, your very existence.

Would your life story represent a philosophy that you would recommend others to read and live by? Sit quietly now and make those corrections. Write the story the way you would like to read it.

Now, it is time to place the title on our book. Think about what you would call your life story. I called mine simply "Fragments." For I felt my life was pieces of dreams. Somehow, all the parts, all the people will come together to complete my purpose on Earth to help write the final chapters, for mine has not ended yet. I certainly wish to stay to do the editing and rewriting of the final chapters. What is the title of your book?

QUESTIONS

Over the years, social service jobs have drawn concerned young people into careers of helping others. In time, many of them end up being what some psychologists call "burned out Samaritans." After a few years of listening to other people's problems and trying to help solve them, the psychologists, doctors, ministers, social workers, psychiatrists, and policemen get to the place where they can't take it anymore. To save themselves emotionally, they must quit, stop caring, or readjust.

As Christians, we are likely to experience some of the same frustrations. By our calling, we are to give, to help others, but eventually, we may find ourselves overwhelmed by the complexity, intensity, and sheer volume of human need. We discover that we just can't keep on burying ourselves in all the pain without it getting to us. We, too, have to quit, stop caring, or readjust.

Some have assumed that the Godliest people keep pushing until they just "wear out for the Lord." That may be the case in some circumstances, but in general, the scriptures indicate that we should adjust our service so that we don't unnecessarily and prematurely become "burned out Christians."

"Lord, give us hearts that truly care for those who suffer everywhere, and when their needs overwhelm the soul, may we roll that burden onto you."

A willing heart must always be kept under the control of a wise head. Let's pause and ask ourselves some questions.

Who are you? Where are you going? Are you static? Are you growing? What can you do to make life better? Are you a giver? Are you a getter? Do you think lovingly? Do you act as you feel? Is your life cold and unreal? Finding wisdom is man's highest aim. Living happily is the name of the game.

What can you do to make your life happier? Can we help each other in some way to be happier? Is your problem attitude, mental consciousness, or realities of life? Begin today to work on all of these.

USED CAR DEALERS DILEMMA

I am a used car dealer's fright.
Just a pile of junk down there on the last row.
Sitting there battered and tarnished, watching life go.
When they came with the bill of sale and a truck ready
    to tow,
I knew I was headed for the junk heap.
Scrap iron to be recycled in somebody's jeep.
I started screaming, "You can't have this classy chassis."
I have millions of miles to go.
You need to rebuild the engine, add a new carburetor
and see that the oil can flows.
Polish out the dents, take a tuck in the seats,
four new tires and I will be one of the fleet.
Now I'm a used car dealer's delight.
Look out when I pass you on the freeway, economy cars
    and trucks.
This spruced up hunk of metal flies and struts.
This classy chassis has millions of miles to go.
So hurry get my paperwork signed and let me run solo.

AUTUMN

AUTUMN SERENADE

Autumn is one of my favorite times of the year. It's the time the leaves turn to flame, and the hills are a riot of color. In the crisp autumn air, my thoughts go to covered bridges, like you see in the New England states, gathering wood for the fireplace, and hunting pinecones. It's a time for self-communion.

Autumn is also the start of the holiday season, and holidays are meant for families, for good times, and for remembering what each special holiday means to us.

Thanksgiving will soon be upon us, and a million memories crowd my mind. When I was a little girl, I remember helping mama in the kitchen making pies, cooking cranberries and mincemeat, and helping with the turkey stuffing and the Indian pudding. Now, I do all these things with my own family, and my children are the helpers. Through the years, this feast of the pilgrims has been a special event in our home.

Like everyone else, we look forward to getting the grandparents and all the family together. There are family games that work up a giant hunger and a fabulous meal where everyone eats too much ... but after all, it's a holiday.

When our family and friends gather around the fireplace after dinner, we all thank God for the harvest of love, laughter, health, and work —our home and loved ones. We also exchange our favorite stories of what Thanksgiving means to us.

I think every American knows the story of the Mayflower and the Pilgrim Fathers who came to this country to find the freedom to worship the Lord in the way they thought best. We all know about the first Thanksgiving when those same pilgrims celebrated with their Indian brothers the gifts that God had provided. Every schoolchild knows the Thanksgiving symbols of turkeys, buckle shoes, blunderbusses, high-crowned hats, and pumpkin pie.

All these things are important, but I wonder how many boys and girls or adults can tell you the story of Burial Hill ... and what role it played in the pilgrim's heritage.

Burial Hill is a beautiful slope that stands above Plymouth Harbor. Today, the winds play through the green grass while below, tourists visit Plymouth Rock and go aboard the replica of the Mayflower. However, on that first terrible winter in the new world, Burial Hill claimed over half the little band of people that had fled England to find religious freedom.

In everything great and good, there is a price that must be paid. The pilgrims had left behind family and friends they would never see again, and they made their way to a strange land because the love of God and the right to worship him was greater than all the comforts and security of home. The price they paid was very high. Young mothers and fathers and their children found a final resting place on Burial Hill that first winter.

The half of the pilgrim band that survived climbed high on Burial Hill that day in late spring when the Mayflower sailed for England. As they watched the sails fade from sight in the blue Atlantic, they knew that not a single man, woman, or child who had left Europe for the new world would be returning.

They had found their home. In this sometimes cruel, sometimes beautiful land, they would stay and bring the word of God and the message of the Bible to those who would follow in the years ahead.

Slowly they made their way down Burial Hill. Some stopped to place a wildflower on a mound of clay while others remembered in their hearts the friends who had made the long journey with them, full of hope and the love of God, their friends who had paid the price of seeking religious freedom.

Burial Hill belongs to the ages, part of our past, part of our heritage. A place where a price was paid so that you and I, and all the people who have gone before, and those who will follow, will have the right to worship as they choose, to be free and live free with God in the greatest nation.

Let us not ever forget our heritage.

WEST VIRGINIA STATE OF MIND

I love the hills the trees and the greens
I know that it is probably way beyond my means
It's much too much to put upon my plate
But I want to adopt West Virginia - the entire State.

Others adopt a child or a hound, but I'm West Virginia bound.
I'll take all the people, the good and the bad.
For I have found something special that I've never had.
A West Virginia state of mind that makes me glad.

A place to meditate and never be sad.
A place to be proud of, a delight to visit.
A place to be part of, that's truly exquisite.
A sense of belonging and love.
My adopted State and I fit like a glove.

It's a special rapport, a genuine admiration
A real belonging, a sense of participation.

INSTEAD OF THERAPY

The trees, the ground, the rivers
Are all a medley of glorious givers.
My senses are gone from the world around.
Life is one of stress and worries that abound.
However it leaves me holding a clear vision and sound
Right now it's true, I'm West Virginia bound.

The peace and quiet, the joy and serenity.
The life that seems so full of plenty.
Perhaps I can end my restless search
Find a home of loveliness, my place on earth.

I'm West Virginia bound.
Oh how I love that sound.
Glorious days, endless times of rapport
A West Virginia state of mind comes over me evermore.

How I escape from everyday pressures,
Mentally I travel in words and gestures
To a wondrous place I would love to be.
I want to adopt West Virginia, hurry tell me who must
    I see.
Dear Governor, please hear my plea.

EVANGELISM

Many of us associate evangelization with missionary work in faraway places, or with going door to door preaching a certain doctrine, or preaching from collapsible tents or street corners, or voices blaring out to us from a radio or television sets. Yes, it can be all those things, and much, much more. It is touching lives in a way that people will be changed. That they will recognize and accept Christ's love for themselves. So, anytime we do anything to bring about the kingdom of God in the world today and in people's hearts, we are evangelizing.

Since the Pope's declaration called Vatican II, a new awareness of us, the people of God, as Evangelizers has come about. Now, we are beginning to see filling the needs of people as every real act of evangelizing. We are coming to realize that we have to renew ourselves in order to most effectively reach out to the needy and so speak Christ to the world.

There is good news. God offers eternal life to all mankind through Jesus Christ. Today the Christian community calls you to be an apostle of this good news. An apostle is one who is sent as a commissioned ambassador with the full authority of the sender to proclaim the good news. Your call is to evangelism. To be an ambassador of Christ. God, as it were, appealing through you. The spirit of evangelism flows from the love of God our Father. God sent his son into this world as his apostle of love, divine love. "God so loved the world that he sent his only begotten son. That the world might be saved through him" (Jen. 3 vs. 16). This teaches us that all men and women need to be saved. "Jesus of Nazareth appears on this earth as the supreme apostle of the Father, filled with enduring love" (Jen. 1 vs. 14). "The people of Samurai be held in Jesus the Savior of the world" (Jen. 4 vs. 42).

A recent Gallup poll indicated that 80 million Americans (roughly 38.6% of the total U.S. population) have no religious affiliation. I am sorry to say the state of California ranks much higher than the national average, with 57% of its people being non-churchgoing. We who are evangelized, that is, those of us who are deepening our commitment to Christ and church, must, in turn, become the evangelizers. In order to accomplish this, we, in the church communities, need more growth in knowledge of the Gospels and a great concentration on spirituality.

The above figures are impressive to some, but to many of us, they are awesome. The goal of evangelization, to proclaim the good news to every creature, cannot be accomplished in our local churches alone, but by every person reaching out to a neighbor in trouble, a teenager who has drifted away from the church or from society in general, or a co-worker that has never really stopped to listen to the good news, who might only need a friendly invitation to come to church. In the book *Each New Day*, we are told about what it will be like in heaven. "When you enter the beautiful city, and the saved all around you appear. What joy, when someone will tell you, 'It was you who invited me here.'"

Put your trust in the Gospel of Jesus Christ. The church has had one mission from the very beginning. All churches "Go into the whole world and proclaim the good news to all creation." In a word, we must evangelize. We must proclaim the great works of God in word and deed. Through the testimony our lives give, we must call others to see and acknowledge the mystery of his love, for it is a gift to be shared.

As we grow deeper in our personal conversion, we will begin to see how all of our current efforts are already small parts of our response to Jesus's call to spread the good news. When we pray together and when we pray separately, when we visit the sick and comfort the sorrowing, and feed the poor and inform the curious. When we help others in any way to hear and respond to the call of the Lord, we are evangelizing. While doing all of these things, we must never hesitate to proclaim the message which motivates all these deeds, for the power of that message reaches far beyond the effects we might see.

In 1976 Pope Paul VI re-affirmed this mission of the churches for us again. He urged us again to evangelize. That is to bring the good news into all the strata of humanity. Evangelization is not meant for missionaries alone or ministers alone. For that matter, it is a call from the Lord himself that must touch every man, woman, and child who believes in his name. Evangelism means active concern for our many neighbors who do not believe in God's saving grace. We must put aside our shyness and speak out our faith. Evangelization also means that we must listen more closely to the scriptures and the churches' teaching so that the Lord can draw forth the living Christ-like love that our neighbors need from us each day. It means the dedication to serve, which marks the lives of so many who give their time and energy in the many forms of Christian service. Finally, evangelization means the prayer-filled acceptance of the Lord's call when suffering and grief arise.

Who in the church today does the Holy Spirit call to evangelize? Pope Paul VI also stated, "We wish to confirm once more that the task of evangelizing all people constitutes the essential mission of any church." The whole church is missionary. And the work of evangelization is a basic duty of the people of God. "You, yes you, are called by the holy spirit to be an evangelist. Be an apostle of the Holy Spirit. You will go forth as his ambassador filled with power from on high. You go forth in the name of the Father, the Son, and the Holy Spirit."

When they call you an evangelist, hold your head high and remember you are doing the Lord's bidding. They could be calling you many worst names.

Remember, they once called Jesus a traitor to his church and country. Be proud to be an evangelist.

DESTINY

Start out by trying to be a little kinder
with the passing of each day.
To leave only happy memories
as we go along our way.

To use possessions that are ours
in service full and free.
To sacrifice the trivial things
for larger good to be.

To give of love in lavish ways
that friendship true may live
To be less quick to criticize
more ready to forgive.

To use such talents as we have
that happiness may grow.
To take the bitter with the sweet
assured it is better so.

INSTEAD OF THERAPY

To be quite free from self intent
whatever the task we do.
To help the world's faith in God and right
no matter how things run.

To work and play and pray and trust
until the journeys done.
God grant to us the strength of heart
of motive and of will.

To do our past and falter not
God's purpose to fulfill.

STANLEY FINDS LIVINGSTONE

There are many great moments played on the stage of history, and one of these took place in east Africa in 1871.

No bands played; no cannons were fired. There were no waving banners, and no sabers flashed as armies charged, nor did the world even know about this historic moment in time until weeks after it had happened.

A motion picture producer would never have selected this site for the climax of his multi-million-dollar production. In 1871 television and radio were not factors to be considered, and even the greatest newspapers were sometimes months late in reporting news from the far-flung frontiers.

The heat was unbearable. In the distance, the trumpeting of elephants, the roar of a lion, and the growl of a man-eating tiger blended with the orchestration of wild birds and other jungle creatures. The small red eyes of crocodiles peered just above the green water of the murky swamps, and high in the jungle vines, a boa constrictor watched the scene play out below.

The swamps on two sides and the green walls of the jungle

on the others framed the small clearing where two white men faced each other. Both men looked the worse for wear. Their jungle whites were spattered with swamp mud, and the growth of beards was tangled and dirty. Both men had a small group of natives behind them.

For a few seconds, the men just stared at each other. Then slowly, the taller of the two men moved forward and uttered the words that will go into the pages of history and be repeated again and again as long as history is written or remembered. "Dr. Livingstone, I presume." With this short phrase, one of the greatest searches in history ends.

David Livingstone was a humble mill worker in Scotland when a profound spiritual experience made him resolve to be a medical missionary. Convinced that the God who had called him would see him past all the daunting obstacles in his way, he trained in theology and qualified in medicine. In 1840 he set out for South Africa. When an old missionary from that region spoke of the vast unoccupied district to the north, where on a clear morning one could see the smoke of a thousand villages that no missionary had ever been before, Livingstone's destiny was sealed.

He went north, beyond even the fearsome Kalahari Desert. He learned languages. Got to know the native mind and ventured into places unknown to white men. His scientific notes led to his being acclaimed on his two furloughs in England. On his return to Africa, he dropped from sight, and it was then that the New York Herald sent Henry Stanley on his world-famous search.

Stanley found Livingstone reduced to a living skeleton. He had suffered prolonged hardship and sickness. Stanley spent four months with the veteran explorer and wrote that "his religion ... is a constant, earnest, sincere practice. It governs his conduct not only towards his native servants but towards the bigoted peoples of Africa and all who come in contact with him."

It was a sad day when the two men shook hands and bid farewell. Stanley headed back to America to write the story of this great man, and Livingstone went back to his missionary work with his adopted people.

Two years later, David Livingstone was found dead early one morning. Kneeling by his bed in a native hut. His African attendants carried his body 1500 miles to the coast, where it was sent to England for burial in Westminster Abbey.

David Livingstone regarded himself in God's plan as one of the "watchmen of the night who worked when all was gloom." It was surely fitting that he passed away in the land of endless day, just as dawn was about to break over the Dark Continent.

PEARL

In the sea's depths a pearl was born,
On a high rock a violet blue.
Deep in the cloud a drop of dew.
And in my dreams, you.

The pearl died in a royal crown.
In a fine vase died the withered flower,
Mid snow perished the drop of dew.
And in my dreams, you.

SPIRITUALISM

Spiritualism is the communication of spirit to living humans. Inspiration, or the influx of ideas and prompting from the spirit world, is not a miracle of a past age but a perpetual fact. The ceaseless method of infinite intelligence for human elevation.

The Bible makes many and varied, frequent references to spirits. In the Bible, spirits are also called angels. They are and can be one and the same. From Genesis to Revelations, the nearness of the spirit world and the intercommunication of spirits and mortals runs like a golden strand through the Bible.

Not only spirit communication but every phase of the manifestation distinctively known as modern spiritualism is represented on many occasions. Often hundreds of years apart. This similar expression shows that the same psychic laws held true then as now, whereby mysteries of the Bible and its miracles are explained with a clearness that commentators have not been able to attain for want of knowledge. Angels are understood to be special creations and spirits to have ascended through mortal bodies. The words are used by the writers of the Bible as interchangeable. Such as the following examples: Rev.

I—"the soul of man separated from his body is known as spirit." From Psalm 4, it says, "He maketh his angels spirits." Luke, Chapter 15 refers to departed spirits as "being on the same level with Angels. Neither can they die anymore, for they are equal unto the angels." I understand now why I would like to call my mission the Ministry of Angels. (The Ministry of Spirit).

In Corinthians, Chapter 44, it states that there is a natural body and a spiritual body. How much clearer can it be said?

What spiritualism is and does:

It teaches personal responsibility for all humanity to the individual as growth and development unfold.

It removes all fear of death, which is really the lesson of the spirit world.

It teaches that death is not the cessation of life but merely a change of condition.

It teaches not that man has a soul, but that man is a soul and has a body. That as man sows on Earth, he bears in the life to come.

That those who have passed on are conscious, not asleep.

That communication between the living and the dead is scientifically proved and demonstrated.

It thus brings comfort to the bereaved and alleviates sorrow.

Spiritualism is the science, philosophy, and religion of continuous life. Based upon the demonstrated fact of communication, by means of mediumship, with those who live in the spirit world.

It brings to the surface man's spiritual gifts, such as inspiration, clairvoyance, clairaudience, and healing powers.

It teaches that the spark of divinity dwells in all.

That as a flower gradually unfolds in beauty, so the spirit of man unfolds and develops in the spirit spheres.

Spiritualism is God's message to mortals, declaring that there is no death. That all who have passed on still live.

That there is hope in the life beyond for the most sinful.

That every soul will progress through the ages to heights, sublime and glorious, where God is love and love is God.

It is a manifestation, a demonstration, and proof of the continuity of life and the truth of the many spirit manifestations recorded in the Christian Bible.

It demonstrates the many spiritual gifts mankind is endowed with but which, throughout want of knowledge, have been allowed to lie dormant or, through prejudice, have been violently and unjustly suppressed.

Now you know what it does.

What spiritualists believe:

Express belief in a supreme impersonal power everywhere present, manifesting as life, through all forms of organized matter. Called by some God, by others as spirit, and in some cases, called infinite intelligence.

In this manner, we express our belief in the immanence of spirit and that all forms of life are manifestations of spirit or infinite intelligence, and thus that all people are children of God.

In conclusion, I wish to share an affirmation that I particularly like, which states the psychology of spiritualism without really saying that word.

I think you will find it uplifting and spiritual. I am expressing God.

As the expression of God, I possess the ability to become conscious of all knowledge, the higher knowledge, and wisdom, for God is all-knowing and possesses all wisdom and knowledge.

I am one with God, and I must acknowledge this fact through the continual and progressive application of myself in fulfilling my duties to my fellow man in my demonstrations of my oneness with God, the mind, the love, the wisdom, and the sense of true being and life and all the beauties of life.

I am God expressed, and as the expression of God, I possess the ability to become conscious of and use this wonderful omnipotent power of love and life. In demonstrating my oneness with God.

WINTER

YULETIDE SEASON

The Yuletide season is upon us. It is the time for Christmas trees, heavy snows, and logs burning in the fireplace. In California, it's a time for sunshine, decorated palm trees, and Christmas bells ringing on the streets and in the church towers. The time for peace on Earth and goodwill toward men. Most important, it's a time for reunion, to get together within the family circle and feel once more the warmth and love that can be found only when the family is together.

It is this time of year when more than any other, you will find the two most important words in the English language on the lips of everyone you meet, the magic words "Going Home."

Home—that word is uttered, and a million thoughts flash into the mind. Home—mother, father, and the folks that mean so much to us. Home—thoughts of happy days and of memories of other holiday seasons.

To each of us, home means something different. It may be a big mansion on a hill or the humble home of a mill worker. It may boast the finest furniture money can buy, or maybe there is a darn in the clean tablecloth, and the rug is worn in spots. These things are immaterial, for no matter whether you are rich or poor, mighty or meek, home is home, and there is no other place like it in the world.

It is where you played your childhood games, where you came with your sorrow and joys. It is where your minor achievements were looked upon as giant successes and where, when you failed, you were told that this was only a temporary setback and that you would triumph in the end.

You walk into your old room and notice that it hasn't changed. There hangs the picture of your high school friends or a picture of a school team on which you played, and in a special frame is a single picture of that someone special, a dream date. It seems ages since you last saw that person.

You can smell the good aroma of food cooking, drifting up from the kitchen, and you can hear your mother humming as she works, just like she always used to.

A million memories flood over you as you sit at the dinner table thinking about the old times and recalling the friends of yesteryear.

In the evening, as you sit in your favorite easy chair with your old dog or cat curled up at your feet or in your lap, you forget the cares of the world, for you are in that world of enchantment known as the home place.

Yes, this is the Christmas season, the pine trees, colored lights, the carolers with the age-old songs of "Silent Night" and the "The First Noel." These are the part of the pageantry of Christmas.

This is a time for joy, love, and goodwill. This is the time for going home, the time to enter once more into the family circle and to recapture the glory and true spirit of Christmas.

As you walk down the street in the early morning, you will

perhaps think you glimpse some of the faces of those who have gone on. Or maybe you will arrive in the old town when the streetlights are casting their soft glow upon the snow-covered streets, and you see the lamps burning in the windows like beacons to guide the wayfarer. There will be a few moments of sadness, but this will be dispelled when you walk by the white picket fence and put your hand on the front gate. You will gaze at the old home, and you can't help but brush away a tear or two.

This year, when you stand before the Christmas tree, put your arm around your Mom and tell her how much you love her and how swell it is to be home. Tell Dad how you enjoyed his letters and have one of those heart-to-heart talks, just like old times.

When you kiss that girl or guy under the mistletoe. Let them know how much you care, and no doubt they have words of love to express also.

Yes, by all means—Go Home. Home, where the heart is, where love springs eternal, and where the old story of the Christmas legend is the sweetest.

But for many of us, there is no "Going Home." For home and family are no longer there. However, we can be thankful for wonderful memories and reflections. We can return home in our minds, remember our loved ones. And say a special blessing that the Lord guides, guards, and protects them through eternity.

As we approach Christmas day, lift up your eyes to the great meaning of the day and dare to think of your humanity as something so divinely precious that it is worthy of being made an offering to God.

Count it as a privilege to make that offering as complete as possible, keeping nothing back, and then go out to the pleasures and duties of life, having been truly born anew into his Divinity, as he was born into our humanity on Christmas day. Experience all the wonderful blessings of the Christmas season. May each of us, in our own special way ... Go Home.

CHRISTMAS

Let us pray that strength and courage abundant be given to all who work for a world of reason and understanding, that the good that lies in every man's heart may day by day be magnified, that men will come to see more clearly, not that which divides them, but that which unites them, that each hour may bring us closer to a final victory, not of nation over nation, but of man over his own evils and weaknesses, that the true spirit of this Christmas Season—its joy, its beauty, its hope, and above all it abiding faith —may live among us, that the blessings of peace be ours—the peace to build and grow, to live in harmony and sympathy with others, and to plan for the future with confidence.

WHAT IS CHRISTMAS

The merriest day. The saddest day. The day that you are happiest over all you have had. The day that your heart aches most for all that you have missed or have had and lost. That's Christmas. The day that sets you tingling with joyous anticipation for weeks beforehand. The day you wish you could sleep straight through and thus wipe off your calendar. That's Christmas. The day that rouses in you all that is generous and tolerant and kindly. The day that wearies you with sentimentality and disappointment and despair ... that's Christmas.

Christmas is like the illusion produced by the East Indian fakir. There he squats in the dust, waving a bright-colored rag. One onlooker sees a star of hope. Another, a tree glittering with gifts, another an octopus of bills squeezing and crushing, another nothing.

But stop, have not all of us helped to maintain the illusion, by our willingness to accept as true whatever seemed to take form and shape out of the dust?

More than that, are not we ourselves responsible for some

of the imaginary creations that obscure the beautiful reality of Christmas.

There is the story of Santa Claus. Kindly intentioned but nevertheless a myth. A continual feeding of the child's excitement by references to what he may get. Always what he is likely to receive? Rarely what he ought to give. The child, wearied by all the unaccustomed excitement and adjusting to so many new things or sensing the emptiness of the gift-less days to follow Christmas, has his first taste of disappointment.

Then suddenly, he slips over the line. He is no longer a child to take such pleasure in receiving. He must learn to rejoice in giving. And to find gratification in giving whether or not he has a keen personal interest in the recipient. Because until he has done that, every broken family tie, every disappointment in human relationships will recur in memory at Christmas time to make it a season of regret. Or suppose he has the loved one and wants to give, oh, so much more than his pocketbook will afford. He measures his ability to be generous in dollars. Whereas there are a hundred things any of us would prefer to the most expensive jewel. The promise of a hundred smiles throughout the year to come. The pledge from a chronic worrier to stop fretting. The assurance from a secretive person that he will share the troubles that otherwise might lead to baffling behavior.

But, you say, these are not gifts for Christmas. No. They cannot be wrapped in colored paper and tied with tinsel cord or ribbon, but they will outlast many. So many legends have sprung up around the day that it is sometimes difficult to separate fact from fancy. There is the story, for instance, of the humble woodcutter who had cut green branches for his hovel but had nothing with which to beautify those branches for his children's joy. Then in the snow, he found a child shivering in his rags. Hungry for want of food. The woodcutter brought the child to the warmth of his fire and gave him his own supper. By morning, the child had vanished, but there on the branches was a web of light. Just such a blaze of gold and silver as many happy fingers will be tracing over thousands of trees on Christmas eve this year.

But the woodcutter received because he gave, not in exchange for a gift expected in return. But to a helpless child whose need he served—thus making him indeed one of those special people who will serve the father's work first of all in their lives.

There is one symbol that we know related directly to that first Christmas. The gifts which we stuff into stockings, pile under trees, send through the mail, or carry ourselves to our friends are the sign of those other presents of gold and frankincense and myrrh which the wise men of the east laid beneath the star at the feet of the baby in the manger. But they were "wise men." They did not give to each other, but to one they hailed as the master.

What a Christmas this would be for the whole world if every one of us would wrap up that secret worry. The resentment, that bit of black depression, impatience, malice, or hatred we have carried around willingly or unwillingly with us for so long. And having wrapped it up, that we should place it at the feet of the Christ child and go away and leave it there to be transformed into a priceless offering of self-sacrifice and self-abnegation.

And if in the same secret altar place of our hearts, we should lay down the bits of patience, kindness, and gentleness we should like to pass on to others all this year, that they, too, may be magnified and glorified by contact without the highest sense of good.

To do this would be a celebration worthy of the one whose anniversary day it is. To do this would bring to ourselves joy and satisfaction and peace. For Christmas is to each of us just what we make it.

Let us pray that strength and courage in abundance be given to all who work for a world of reason and understanding that the good that lives in every man's heart may day by day be magnified, that men will come to see more clearly not that which divides them but that which unites them. That each hour may bring us closer to a final victory, not of nation over nation, but of man over his own evils and weaknesses, That the true spirit of this Christmas season, its joy, its beauty, its hope and above all its abiding faith, may live among us that the blessings of peace be ours ... the peace to build and grow. To live in harmony and sympathy with others and to plan for the future with confidence.

SOFTWARE SANTA CLAUS

A child sits before the screen
mesmerized by what he's seen
Santa's jumping over rooftops
Reindeer flying without stops
Colored packages piled high
Santa driving with a sigh
Java Santa's set an all time record
Children logging on in droves
Oops, there he goes topping orange groves.
Gently landing on a sprawling roof
Down the chimney without a goof
Stopping to leave a message on E-mail
Taking time to write one in Braille
Searching for the tree, tasting a candy
Knowing that he must get handy
Spreading packages all around
Do it quick without a sound
Oops, here's Fido tearing up the ground
Up the chimney to the next place

Who knows what Santa might embrace?
Software Santa's back in the race
Hurry now, must keep the pace.
He's on the screen and in our vision.
Set about his Christmas mission.
Santa's not all time and space.
He's in our heart and everyplace.
Oops, screen two just got erased.
Software Santa is joy and fun
A visual game for kids on the run
Hurry, hurry the games quite clear.
No computer glitches here.
Speeding reindeer, one last round,
On to the North Pole, back to the ground.
Faster, faster there is nothing to fear.
Dawn is breaking, daylight starting here.
Oops, Christmas Day, then New Year.

FINDING THE RIGHT CHURCH

A group of gentlemen was discussing church. Their church wasn't what they thought it should be. It was not the perfect model of perfect Christians. Since it wasn't what it ought to be, they were considering joining another one.

Suppose you aren't satisfied with your present church, and there is not another one around that is satisfactory, either. Then what? Should you start a new one?

Many Christians are confronted and entangled with these questions. Often, out of reaction to something in our background, we become sure our church isn't the right one. Natural inclinations are to take lessons from others who join and rejoin in search of the right church in which souls are being saved.

We do seem to have a built-in instinct to want to rally behind "where the action is." This sometimes becomes the deciding factor for which is the right church, but action and perfection are two different things. This calls for a decision of deeper values.

As for myself, I've given up on the search for a perfect

church. Why? First, each group is made of about the same stuff. They are human beings. Holy as some say they are, they still show their human colors. I have been in many kinds of churches and personally listened to the problems of their members. When all the boiling is over, they still have human conflicts.

Second. The search for the perfect church will keep me occupied for life. When our life, which is like a moment, is over, it will have been spent looking for the right church with the right people to suit our taste. Many Christians waste their lives going from church to church, causing strife and confusion as they go. There must be a more valuable search for us.

Third. The real question is missed in uptight discussions about finding a perfect church. We fail to ask how to become the perfect person to make the perfect church. This is the crucial point. Becoming the right kind of person. It isn't finding the right church but being the right kind of person in the church.

My concern now is whether or not I am becoming the right person after all. I am a part of the church, and it is foolish for me to push all the blame of imperfection onto others. So, the real task for each individual is to seek to become the person God meant for us to be when he created us.

Now my real task is to start being everything I think a church ought to be. Better yet, to reach to become what Christ wants his church to be. When this begins, fulfillment and purpose in life take place. Then, the person becomes an optimistic, happy child of God who lives with enthusiasm for Christ. He will not be the negative person who sees everything everyone else does as doomed. Who can hardly wait for God to pour out judgment on the sinners around him.

There are a few things involved in becoming the right church. If I want to be a part of a church that isn't always having trouble, I'll have to be a peacemaker instead of a troublemaker. If I'm not part of the solution, I am part of the problem. If it is to be a mission church, it must begin with people. It must begin with me. I must stop crying about others and go to work myself. Those who cry the loudest are often working the least. Instead of expecting others to be the model church, my challenge is to personally become that model.

Where do I go from here to be the church? One, I center attention on being the right kind of person. I best become that person by giving up my selfish desires and giving my life to Christ and his cause. As the Bible points out ... present your bodies a living sacrifice ... I must sacrifice my will and vow to do his will.

Two. I work to be a person through whom God's love can flow to others. My goal will be to become a giving person. Giving of myself—love, compassion, talents, and blessings to others. I'll ask, "What can I give?" Not "What can I get?" It is more blessed to give than to receive. Invest your life in a person.

Three. I'll be a Christian during conflict. Instead of blaming others for the conflict. I will first check out myself. Correcting any trace of the problem. Conflicts will be present. I'll accept the challenge of working through them instead of around them. I must be willing to ask, "Give, and receive forgiveness." I'll go sin hunting in my own woods first.

Four. To be the church, I must practice a meaningful ministry. God doesn't call his children to a ministry of tearing down the character and ministry of fellowmen. I don't recall reading in the Bible of a ministry of criticism such as some Christians keep nursing. We must go to something constructive. Discovering the true purpose of ourselves. And giving encouragement to others. Cheer up and smile. The work of Christ is the greatest and highest calling in the world.

Finally, joining the church isn't a free ride to glory. It is a public expression of my standing with God and his people. It has a commission to keep. Keeping that commission should be my aim.

To me, being the church means to stop searching and start building. Stop complaining and start working. Stop grumbling and start witnessing. In my experience, the work of the church in the seventies and eighties and nineties begins as ... I give myself to investing in persons for Christ's sake.

So, instead of joining and unjoining in a search to find the perfect church, consider how can I become the Church? How can I become the best that God wants me to be? Tell God, from this day on, I'm yours. I'll do your will and yield to your word. Make me into the church you want. When a man starts becoming his best for God, the question of finding the right church will begin to answer itself.

HYPE

Most of you know that I work in the film business. I spend several hours a day at the major film studios involved in one picture or another. Recently at a meeting, the conversation swung around to the rating of pictures—G, PG, R, and X—and then the conversation turned to X-rated pictures and pornography.

At this point in the conversation, my mind started wandering as X-rated pictures hold very little interest for me. However, my mind began to think of the ultimate pornography: X-mas, the abbreviation for Christmas.

The shimmer and glitter of Christmas are all gone now. Garlands hang askew, and store lights no longer twinkle. Santa Claus is back on the unemployment line. Storekeepers are home counting the take. Shoppers are left with empty pockets, overdrawn checking accounts, and overcharged credit cards.

"The Hype," as I call it, started before Thanksgiving. We were hit with Christmas commercials on radio and television every few minutes. We didn't turn them off. We watched. We listened. We bought. We surrendered to commercialism.

Passive, indifferent, and uncaring, while big business rewrote the storyline. But we can't blame the merchants. They hang Christmas decorations in October because we accept them. God help us, we gave in without a fight. No talking back. No letters to Congressmen. No complaints to TV programmers. Nothing. Not a word.

And in most cases, not a word to our children. We surrender them to the red-suited jolly old giver of gifts and the flop-eared bearer of sweets. Maybe there was a Christmas show or two at a neighborhood church, but how many kids attended? If there was a program about Christmas at school, it wasn't likely about a baby or a manger.

It's no wonder the kids talk about other superheroes. Superman, Iron Man, The Incredible Hulk. They get these in their diet 52 times a year—maybe more, with reruns. Ten to one, they can tell you much more about how Superman saved the world than they can about the One sent to a manger to "seek and save that which was lost."

A babe in swaddling clothes? Hardly the impact of a Superman costume. That's the way, as a superhero, his contemporaries thought Jesus was going to come—as a conquering hero to save them from the Roman yoke. But he, Jesus, came to save mankind from far more than the tyranny of an earthly kingdom. He came to save the world from sin. "Behold the Lamb of God that taketh away the sin of the world," said John the Baptist.

Quite a story, really. Much more impressive than the feat of the red-suited miracle worker who flies without wings and slips down chimneys, knows all, and sees all. You know him as Santa Claus. There'll be another Christmas. Another chance for all of us to remember that he, Jesus, came first. We didn't have a Christmas before he came.

It seems like the ultimate pornography to X-rate it. Like in

X-mas. Pornography that can't be undone by substituting other names, as in Supermas, Santamas, Ironmas, or Hulkmas. There's only one name that really fits, like in Christ-mas. And that, it seems, was what he was trying to get across all along.

Jesus could use your help next December, and if I heard that last commercial right, that's only "---" shopping days away. Time to swing into action now. Remember, next year, let's not relate Christmas by the letter "X" in X-mas. That's really the ultimate pornography—to treat Jesus's birthday that way. It's worse than the lowest porno film. For even the highest-grossing dollar film in porno only lasts two or three years. Yet we have misspelled Christ's birthday year in and year out, abbreviating it, commercializing it, and flagrantly misleading our children into not realizing the real reason we celebrate the day.

I know this topic probably seems out of time. It's not in December; no, it's not Christmas. But the advertising agencies with which I deal are already planning the campaign, starting to film the sequences, the commercials, the movies that will be shown next Christmas to hype the market to get you to feel jovial, happy, and family-minded. But the subliminal message is to get you to spend your dollars. For without your cooperation, this commercialized promotion of the giving of gifts, of buying beyond your means, could not be culminated.

You know the tremendous commercial hype is applied to all the holidays. We are presently approaching St. Patrick's Day, and very shortly after that will be Easter. How many of you buy gifts for family, for children, for grandchildren? Perhaps we should stop and, instead of buying something, decide we are going to show our love this year in a different way. Share something you already own. Give a cooked specialty. Give time and service to help someone. There's a number of ways to reach out and show love. We don't have to be pushed into buying, and more buying, especially in these times where the economy is terrible and prices are soaring.

Working in the industry and seeing so many lies perpetrated on the American public eventually seems to get you. I have watched writers and producers destroy history and create characters that were totally different. Frequently, we were led to believe that they were good on television, when in fact, they were bad. For instance, the story of Wyatt Earp. Several years ago, a series was created to show Wyatt Earp as a great gunslinger, the hero of the west. However, he was an outlaw who frequently shot people in the back. Unfortunately, the writer and producer didn't tell us the real story.

Yesterday, I turned on the television in the afternoon for a brief period, which I never do. However, it was just in time to see a band of Indian braves of the old west dancing with white women from a nearby town. This sequence was part of a story where the women frequently visited the Indian camp and helped with food and medicine for the Indian children. Well, I can guarantee in history you would never find any true statements where white women danced with the Indians and had parties and teas. The only time the Indians danced was after they had been drinking and almost always just before a battle.

I am tired of these flagrant types of abuses. I think it would be much better for all of us to rate programs, television, and movies by fiction and truth or fact ratings. Then at least, we would have a chance to know and decide what we wish to absorb in our minds. For the mind is a giant sleeping computer that can be programmed with evil or falsehoods and eventually believes it as truth. All children tend to believe each new thing that they learn as truth. We need to watch closely what each new generation is absorbing, for eventually, they will be running the country with their ideas and ideals.

It's strange how one's mind can ramble on when it wishes to tear off a subject that it finds unappealing. All this started with the thoughts of X-rated pornography, which I personally see as an appalling sign of our times.

PAY THE PRICE

Pay the price; it's worth it. Jesus began his ministry by calling people to follow him. He said to Andrew and Peter, "Follow me." That call has been going on ever since—today, his spirit calls people to follow him and carry on his work. Jesus said that "He that taketh not his cross, and followeth after me is not worthy of me."

What does it mean to follow Jesus and be his disciple? For Andrew and Peter, it meant leaving the fishnets and accepting another way of life. What does it mean for us to be disciples today? What is the price of discipleship? Let's say you are a Jewish boy. You were taught the laws of God and that Messiah would soon come. You went through Jewish school, attending the synagogue every Sabbath. Keeping the holidays and deeply treasuring your bar mitzvah service. Your ties are close to your family. Then contact with a follower of Jesus happens. You're told of Christ's love, death, and resurrection, that he was wounded for our transgressions. You yield your life to Jesus and through him as your savior. The news reaches your family. You are an outcast. Rejected as a son. A mock funeral is held for you. Would you follow Christ if that were you? Today people are still doing this in some families.

For a Jewish person to become a disciple of Jesus often means rejection by his family. Loss of all he holds dear to himself and a complete change of living. It is a costly thing for a Jew. Another example is that suppose you lived in a country that forbade the public expression of religion, except at the government-approved church. As a result of Christians privately sharing with you, you become a follower of Jesus. You ask to be baptized into their fellowship of believers. You are in the meeting, and just as you are being baptized, some strangers break through the door. You are captured, imprisoned, and tortured because you chose to follow Jesus. Can you imagine being a follower of Jesus like that?

For some people, following Christ means making a change in their lives. They know the cost of discipleship is high. For others, the sacrifice of self is the price they pay. What does it mean to the twenty-first century American to follow Christ? Often, it seems the American image of a Christian is that of someone from a good family who bothers no one, has a good income, provides well for his family, and pays his church dues. He gives his out-of-style clothes to the Salvation Army. Thanks God once a year for his freedom in a Christian nation.

He occasionally occupies a pew and smiles at the pastor as he goes out the door. Is that being a disciple? No. That makes Jesus too cheap. He is not just a blesser of our system. Following him is not having him bless our wealth and approve of our self-indulgence while the rest of the world suffers. He is another way of life. He is another kingdom.

Being a disciple is more than a TV star referring to God at the end of a show. It is more than thanking God for helping our team win the ball game. More than singing a hymn after an all-night jamboree. It is more than wearing a love pin, or a smile button, or decorative clothing.

Being a disciple is following Jesus. It is not Jesus following us. Blessing the stock market so we can hoard up more possessions. It does mean we give our life, time, money, and talents to him. We accept his orders for our life rather than ordering him.

A journey through the gospels indicates that being a disciple means following Jesus in a radically different way from the world. It is either Jesus or money, God or mammon, one way or another ... broad is the way to destruction ... narrow is the way ... unto life. It is life amid God's enemies. Jesus said I send you forth as sheep in the midst of wolves. It is not a life of popularity. "Ye shall be hated of all men for my name's sake."

Since God has blessed us with freedom of speech and the free enterprise system, shouldn't we indulge and enjoy it? Many Christians justify their overindulgence by saying that God blessed them, so they should enjoy it. This reasoning, beside the teachings of Jesus, leaves me uncomfortable. It makes the call of Christ too cheap. Yes, we should enjoy our blessings and use them in honor of Christ, but not misuse them to satisfy our selfish desire.

With all our wealth, freedom, comfort, and self-sufficiency, how does one become a disciple of Jesus in such a rich culture? Become a hermit and hide in the mountains? Live poorly? No. This does not make you a disciple.

The first step in becoming a disciple is putting oneself on God's altar and yielding our will to doing his will. Saying, "God, here is my life. Use it." When we honestly yield ourselves to follow Christ, then our time, money, and talents become his. They go along to the altar of sacrifice to God.

On the point of time and freedom, American Christians are always busy rushing to and from, but doing what? There are many activities Christians can get involved in, good activities, yet not always are they giving God the best stewardship of their time. Being a disciple means proper use of time, letting God use it to bring hope and love to others. It may mean giving up some good things to do God's work. My time is not mine but God's.

Another crucial point, money. Some Christians say that because God gave them money, they are entitled to enjoy fine cars, around the world trips, and mansions with all the trimmings. They should recognize it all came from God and thank him for it.

I don't recall reading anything like that in the Sermon on the Mount. Being a 21st-century disciple means turning your money into Christian service. It means keeping what you need but not measuring your needs by the Joneses and the Smiths or others in the rat race. It means we remember the lost souls and hunger pains of others. Spend our money on being a disciple of Jesus. There is a challenge. A friend made a great deal of money; however, he and his family lived very simply. Using much of their income for the Lord's work. Now that is being a disciple.

Another test of discipleship is the use of talents. The disciple of Jesus will open his life to him, permitting Jesus to make him into a useful person in today's world. He doesn't reserve his talents for selfish purposes and useless hobbies. He allows the Holy Spirit to make him into a person interested in the needs of others.

The disciple of Jesus will use the free enterprise system, free-floating money, freedom of speech, and freedom of worship to know Jesus. He will turn these blessings into opportunities. He will not devour them selfishly but will use them to build God's kingdom. Are you willing to pay the price of discipleship? To follow Jesus, to live God's plan? It may be costly, but the rewards are eternal.

Pay the price; it's worth it.

NAME OF THE GAME

Who are you? Where are you going?

Are you Static? Are you growing?

What can you do to make life better?

Are you a giver? Are you a getter?

Do you think lovingly? And act as you feel.

Finding wisdom is man's highest aim.

Living with God is the Name of the Game.

WHAT IS LIFE

What is life about, and why am I here? What do I want to become? Do I want to serve or be served? Whom shall I serve? As I look at these questions, I need answers to get on with living. I must know why I am here, whom I am committed to serving, and who leads my life.

Many times, people say, "If only I could live my past over, I'd be different. I would live life with a more correct behavior." I catch myself entertaining the same thoughts sometimes. But Life, like a spoken word, cannot be relived. We must move on to living from where we are. We are free to change our future. Free to examine our commitments. Free to look at our priorities. I've discovered that agonizing over the past, nursing bitterness over failures, and missing out on relationships with others prevents me from joyfully living life.

It is easy to get stuck in the groove of the everyday grind. We may be unaware that life has become miserable because of being stuck in bitterness and resentment. The good news is that there is forgiveness for the past. We are invited to live now. Let's get on with living the way we were designed to live.

Perhaps you, too, may want to get on with living and leave the arguing to others. The man, who lives life with a spirit of love and joy in Christ, says more to his fellowmen than one with an argumentative testimony. So, perhaps you would like to join me in reaching to become a person who draws people to Christ by a radiant life rather than by arguing them into the right belief. Perhaps together, we can become more like Jesus himself, acting with compassion, understanding, love, and care for others. We can be persons alive in Christ doing his will, going on joyously living for him. Let's get on with living.

History tells us that before Columbus discovered America, Spanish coins had stamped upon them the outline of the straits of Gibraltar. Underneath was the Latin inscription "Ne Plus Ultra," meaning "no more beyond." But when the great explorer returned from his voyage to America, new coins were issued which read, "Plus Ultra" simply "more beyond," indicating the reality that there was indeed more world beyond the Straits of Gibraltar in Spain.

Likewise, when Christ went through the narrow passage of death, some thought he would never come back. But three days later, he arose victoriously and promised a fuller life in eternity for all who put their trust in him. His resurrection provides a sure hope for the believer that the "best is yet to come."

Yes, there is "more beyond," the best is yet to come. Let's get on with living. To me, every hour of the day and night is an unspeakable miracle.

ASK FOR WHAT YOU WANT

How to ask God for what we need. God shall supply all your needs according to his riches in glory by Christ Jesus. This powerhouse scripture means exactly what it says. Your needs are all met in Christ Jesus. As revealed in the word, you will discover in Christ the supply of every need of your life. Ask him specifically to meet your need. Then confess it is yours, according to his riches in glory by Christ.

But don't ask him for something today and then come back tomorrow and ask for the same thing in an unbelieving manner. In doing so, you annul your prayer for today.

Praise is the golden key to all the appropriation of the Father's supply for your needs. He has promised ... you have asked him to do it.

Act like he is doing it by praising him.

In your quiet time, ask for whatever you will, praise him, and know that it will come to pass. Then release it.

DON'T LIVE BY THE ADVERTISEMENTS

We are all finding out that living costs are extremely high. Inflation is running rampant. Our dollars do not stretch as far as they use to. Many of us are struggling to pay bills and keep current with our regular expenses.

With these thoughts in mind, I dreamed of an article called "Don't Live by the Advertisements." "We just want to make you happy," the car dealer says after he has convinced you that your present automobile is hopelessly lacking in the necessary conveniences. You simply must buy that new model in his showroom in order to attain proper self-respect.

A funeral director says, "You must lay them away in the very best you can afford." One advertiser says, "Brand A is most effective." "Brand B is more convenient saves time and work," claims another. "You'll be happier with Brand C," says still another.

And so it goes, as advertisers debate and compete in an attempt to get us to buy their products—whether we need them or not.

Are you living by the advertisements? The following are some scriptural guidelines to help us draw our spending into a clear perspective.

First, "Seek ye first the kingdom of God, and his righteousness and all these things (the necessary things) shall be added unto you." Do kingdom buying. Does what you are buying have anything to do with God's kingdom? Does the spending supply a need or is it merely to satisfy your ego? Before you buy, consider God. Put Him first.

Second, "Love God with all your heart, mind, and soul." Can you imagine what would happen if church members put their time, energy, and money to work for God because of love for Him? Just think what kind of community that would be.

Third, Learn contentment. St. Paul said, "I have learned ... to be content." His contentment didn't come from things but from personal faith in God. While the world is striving for more wealth to buy the best comforts and to enjoy the most pleasures, we really need contentment.

Everyone should learn to trust in God to supply their needs. Your energy should be channeled into service for God rather than being expended to gain more materially. Americans become discontent in comparing themselves with society. If we must compare, then let's compare our luxuries with what exists in less privileged parts of the world. Learn to be content with less.

Fourth, keep the focus heavenward. "From whence also we look for the Savior." Our way of life is from heaven. We are citizens of heaven. We would do well to pay more attention to that citizenship and less to temporal things.

Differences that divide us are often caused by our discontentment with another's wealth. Our conversation centers on who is making the cash and how. The money-maker is projected as the real man, while the materially poor but spiritually rich individual is made to look like a welfare tagalong. This breeds discontent and breaks down the equality of brotherhood.

To be a disciple means giving God our undivided loyalty. He must be our way of life. No divided attention on time, money, and possessions. No using Him merely as a first-class ticket to heaven. He wants all of us.

The enemy of God wants to make us uncomfortable, so we will give him the attention and loyalty that belong to God alone. Then, instead of showing loyalty to God, we make things, possessions, our God. Instead of trusting, we watch the stock market rather than being content with the basic needs of life. We seem always to want more. But there is more to life than the endless struggle to obtain material things. Real living is found in yielding to God and serving Him with all our heart, mind, and strength.

I refuse to let the advertisers tell me when I need a new car. When my present car doesn't serve me anymore, then I'll start looking for a replacement. I don't want them commanding my wardrobe. When my shoes wear out, I'll look for something practical, comfortable, and proper to wear. After all, I'm dressing in His honor.

My life is not dedicated to keeping the system going but rather to God, who has led me into freedom from the world system. The lifestyle I would like to enjoy is not a burden, but freedom ... freedom from monthly payments. It gives more freedom to move forward with God's work and the important things in life.

I realize that I am not an alcoholic, nor a smoke-aholic, but rather a shopaholic. A compulsive buyer. Whenever I am depressed, I buy something because it temporarily makes me feel better. When I have an important date, I buy a new dress for a false sense of security.

I am going to make a commitment not to let the advertisers run my life. I hope you will join with me and not let the advertisers run your life. Be content in God, doing that which pleases Him. Let Him rearrange your values. Then you can be set free. Free to get on with the real living.

SLOW ME DOWN LORD

Slow me down, Lord.
Ease the pounding of my heart.
By the quieting of my mind.
Steady my hurried pace.

With a vision of the eternal reach of time.
Give me, amidst the confusion of my day,
The calmness of the everlasting hills.

Break the tensions of my nerves.
With the soothing music of the singing streams
That lives in my memory.

Help me to know
The magical restoring power of sleep.
Teach me the art of taking minute vacations
Of slowing down.

To look at a flower;

INSTEAD OF THERAPY

To chat with an old friend
or make a new one.
To pat a stray dog;
To watch a spider build a web;
To smile at a child;
Or to read a few lines from a good book.

Remind me each day that the race is not always to the
 swift;
That there is more to life than increasing its speed.
Let me look upward into the branches of the tower oak
And know that it grew great and strong,
Because it grew slowly and well.

Slow me down, Lord.
And inspire me to send my roots deep into the soil of
 life's enduring values.
That I may grow toward the stars of my greater destiny.

NEW YEARS

Has the good news been preserved? In preserving the Bible, many ancient writings have disappeared. Like the men who made them, they have returned to dust and are forgotten. Only fragments remain of most literature of several thousand years ago. But the Bible lives on ... it is just as Peter stated, "for all flesh is like grass, and all its glory is like a blossom of grass: the grass becomes withered, and the flower falls off, but the saying of God endures forever. Well, this is the saying, this which has been declared to you as good news."

The Bible's record in surviving both the ravages of time and the attacks of its enemies is remarkable. There is no question that God saw to it that the "good news" was preserved to guide us through the present critical days. The inspired writers recorded the original little books on material made from animal skins. Faithful men saw to it that such early records were preserved safely at the side of the ark, in the sacred box that God commanded the Israelites to make. When Israel fell into "idol" worship, the law as written by Moses was lost for a time, but the good Kind Josiah found it when he was repairing the temple in Jerusalem.

These original writings disappeared at the latest when the Babylonians destroyed this temple in 607 BC. By this time, however, other handwritten copies of these inspired scriptures had been made. History states that God's servant Daniel, a captive in Babylon, was discerned by the books of God's prophecy. That the Jews' captivity would end after minute attention to detail was shown by recopying manuscripts of the Christian Greek scriptures. Thus, we are assured that the Hebrew and Greek texts, from which our modern-day Bibles have been translated, are essentially the same as the original handwritten copies inspired of God. Comparative study of tens of thousands of manuscripts in many languages proves this to be so. Yes, the printed Bible, as we now have it, in over 1,600 languages, is the same word written down by hand under God's inspiration from the sixteenth century B.C.

Millions of dollars each year are spent in buying the current "best sellers," written on every subject known to man and some that are at this time only fantasy.

I wonder how many of you have really read the all-time best seller? With every kind of fact and fiction, fantasy and reality that will ever be known—God's book, the very foundation of our lives, our hopes, and our dreams.

This year, read the greatest "best seller" from cover to cover. In it, you will find the way, the truth, and the light. You will be a better person, and your life will be enriched for your efforts. Make this year's resolution to read the Bible. Truly the greatest story ever told.

SNOWBIRDS

The snow lies light upon my window ledge
While through the cold and wind the snow birds wedge
To leave small footprints in its dazzling white,
So robbing winter of its long dark night.
When through the day all tasks seem strangely vain.
I hug up close to the window pane.
And there is scratched upon the fine cut snows
A love to warm my heart from winter's blows.
For tiny pilgrims with a mission sweet
Have wrought a miracle by slender impressed feet.
So am I taught to trust and brave each blast?
While only snowbirds brought me faith, at last.

LIFE IS A MOST PECULIAR MIXTURE

Life is a most peculiar mixture of joy and sorrow, success and failure, hope and despair, faith and distrust, laughter and tears, ambition and the lack of it, honesty and deceit, sobriety and dissipation, industry and laziness, service to others and selfish consideration of self, and many comparable opposite factors.

To have a well-balanced personality, it is essential that the positive factors are in control and the negative ones rarely get a chance to show their ugly faces. To be a happy individual, it is necessary to make every effort to cultivate the positive factors listed above and to try to eliminate the negative ones. Fortunately, in many respects, we can control what our lives shall be like by how we think, talk, and act. Then, when defeat, despair, and sorrow come—and come they will to all of us—we may have the courage to face them bravely and successfully.

That's a good optimistic philosophy in any man's language.

FAITH

Faith is the trinity.

Faith is the spirit that moves mountains.

Faith is the power and the purity.

Faith is the crown of love - seek ye always those who worship in the love and

the just of their Faith.

This is the positive creative force that inspires the souls of mankind and all living

beings and vibrations of your plane and other planes on your earth.

Seek ye knowledge - the door shall be opened unto Thee.

THE FAULT IS WITHIN

How easy it is to blame others for our failures. No doubt others often make it difficult for us to succeed, but to blame our defeat on others is really to admit that we ourselves are not big enough to overcome the obstacles that are in the way. When the expert misses the mark, he looks for the fault within himself. Failure to hit the bull's eye or to reach the goal is not so much the fault of something beyond us as of something within ourselves. To improve our aim, we must improve ourselves.

To succeed, we must overcome the difficulties and not be overwhelmed by them, for obstacles are but a challenge to the person determined to win. Of many a situation it has been said, it can't be done, "but of every achievement made against insurmountable odds it can be said, 'it couldn't be done, but somehow it was done.'"

MOVING ON—CHURCH CLOSING

Every day the sun sets in the west just as surely as it rises in the east. Every day the water of the sea is evaporated, swept inland to the mountains, and rolls back in streams to the place of its origin. In just this way, all who have shared and learned and loved as part and parcels of this congregation now pass through the doors of this church for the last time, taking with them a little bit of this group. The good times, the bad times, memories of potlucks, bingo parties, psychic fairs, fellowship, and a closer walk with God and love.

During our time together, some have made an almost superhuman effort in working for the church when it seemed they must be too tired to move after working eight or ten hours a day. Others have given of themselves sometimes, and others have just kind of been part of the general scene.

Some of you have journeyed the long and winding path from the little storefront where we did a lot of laughing and crying together. Where, like youth, we felt we could only grow, could only go onto higher things. And we did. At the church on the hill with the new name, we saw progress. We had our inner struggles like all organizations do, but inch by inch, we grew, and although you had to be very patient, the building fund grew. Had we been blessed with the kind of patience our Lord preached about, in time, we could have bought a plot of land and built our own little church. Running a church is really running a business, and even the giants like Ford and Chrysler can make fatal business decisions.

The amazing thing is that it doesn't take a majority to make these changes. Sometimes only one or maybe two malcontents can change the course of history.

When we came to this building, it was a calculated risk. If we failed, we would fail 100%. We could stay where we were and slowly, slowly grow and, in time, have our own house of worship, or we could take the risk, and if we went down, we were through as an organization.

The classes that we were guaranteed never happened. All over the city, many psychic fairs bit the dust as the economy tightened, and we felt the frightening pressure of not having enough money to keep going.

We had made a gigantic error in thinking we were ready to handle a major rental, and the small voices that had urged and pushed for the move went on to greener pastures, leaving the hardcore members with a shell. It is very easy to point fingers. It is very easy to name names, to make acquisitions of whom and why we are closing. I think everyone is looking down the wrong road. How many times I have heard our ministers and other ministers say, "When a door closes, another door opens." Life is really a house of many rooms. When you move into a new room, the door to the old room closes.

Have you ever thought that maybe God has this as a part of our plan? Maybe, together, we have developed on the spiritual path as far as possible. Now, it is time for each of us to seek a new path to spiritual understanding.

I remember just before I graduated from college, I went to my faculty advisor, and I told him I thought I would come back for another year, although I could only take one subject in my major. I had returned to school after the war, and I had found great peace and joy in daily living there. I loved my surroundings and never wanted to leave the boundaries of the campus.

But that wise man realized what was going on inside me, and with his wisdom, he pointed out that I had to leave. There were other worlds ahead, other roads to take, and God had a plan for my life, and I must go out and seek that plan.

Now we are going. Not with sadness, because if there is sadness, then everything done within these walls has been wasted. God is love. God is joy, and if nothing else ... we have found a lot of love together.

Like graduation, some of us will never meet again. Some will keep in touch through the years and some for a little while, and then slip into memory.

The important thing is that we have been so very lucky to be together. To listen to the words of our Lord together, to share the good and the bad, and each of us has grown a great deal, and now we are ready to move on to other things.

As it rises, so sets the sun. It travels to the western horizon and there disappears. To all of you, go with love and with blessings, and know that God will walk with you in the future as he walks with you today.

TOMORROW

Tomorrow. There is no such thing as tomorrow. It is always today. Tomorrow is always coming. Today is the thing we have in our hand, and yesterday is that which we have cast away. Tomorrow is what we are reaching out to grasp. And when we have it in our hand, it is today. Tomorrow is hope; tomorrow is vision. We live for it, and it never comes. In the wink of an eye, we have relinquished today, and what is it we have in its place —tomorrow? No. Today. We drop something in the long path we have traversed; we pick it up eagerly, only to find that it is still what it was yesterday. Today. Tomorrow is just as far off as it was yesterday. It is today for us to live.

COSMIC ORDER

Breathe deeply two or three times and gently relax. Allowing your mind and body to slowly slip away. There comes a time of quietness that seeps through our mortal bodies. It is almost as if, from the core of our beings, a feeling comes through to remind us that we belong to the untroubled cosmic order. Something in us knows that we are greater than any apparent difficulty which may beset us. Now receptive to the universal presence, we somehow sense that no matter what comes our way, we are capable of overcoming it.

This deep intuitive knowledge is the "peace that passes all understanding," the peace that accompanies God's quiet inner voice, which says, "I am here. I am with you," in so many unexplainable ways. It is the peace that lights our way through the valleys of misunderstanding and sorrow until, once more, we arrive at a plateau of spiritual understanding. But like all things spiritual, our peace cannot be forced upon us. Being one of God's gifts to us, it is to be experienced. We began to understand by saying I acknowledge God's preacher in my world this day. I have a deep feeling that tells me all is well by knowing that nothing can disturb this serene quiet core of realization. The divine peace is free to manifest through me so that I become a citadel of tranquility and by knowing that I am happy and grateful to be this instrument of God's expression.

Sit quietly now and recognize and know this feeling, for you can experience it at any time anywhere.

Unused to this new level of thinking, our subconscious mind may simply not believe us for a while. But we must be persistent in our efforts to convince it that we are sincere. Just as a glass of muddy water is clarified by adding drops of crystal clear water, so are the reactions of our subconscious mind. The mind is made more perfect as we drop into it one pure thought after another. I am one with the mind of God. Unbound from past negation. I turn my attention to that which is Godlike. Expanding opportunities, new friends, and a greater happiness are mine. For I accept this new beginning and know that unexpected delights await me. I welcome my good, as I welcome this new day. Attuned to God's inspiration. Divine order is established in my thought. My trust is in God's pure ideas, and I am kept in perfect peace.

THE LAWS

Thou shalt honor and obey thy Father God.
Magnify this force and bring it on the earth plane and all levels of consciousness.
Thou shalt teach the progression of mankind and the fall and the rise of his Kingdom.
Thou shalt write and walk the path of righteousness for His name sake and in love and light, the Son's soul marches forward in thee.
Thou salt do unto others as you would have them do unto you in Thy name sake.
Thou shalt work and strive for harmony and justice for all mankind.
Thou shalt hear and obey the Prophets of thy Father God.
Thou shalt be a friend to the plants, the animals and all creeping things that walketh and swineth upon your plane, and by this, thou shalt be redeemed and filled with Joy of the Father God.

JUSTICE

Thou serveth justice when thou seeketh the soul of
    mankind and bring the love principle forward.
Justice is kindliness.
Justice is hope instead of despair.
Justice is knowing rather than being afraid.
Let justice be your guide.
Let the Law and Justice work hand in hand.

A BIT WEARY

Are you very weary? Rest a little bit.
Seek some quiet corner, fold your hands and sit.
Do not let the worries that have grieved you all the day
    haunt this quiet corner; drive them all away
Let your heart grow empty of every thought unkind
That peace may hover over you, and joy may fill your
    mind.
Soon you'll feel so rested, so glad you stopped a bit. In
    this quiet corner, to fold your hands and sit.

FAMOUS QUOTES

In life, all each of us really wants to do is be remembered for doing quality work, for loving God and our family, and for contributing something of lasting value to our countryside.

I am involved in a freedom ride protesting the loss of the minority rights belonging to the few remaining earthbound stars. All we demanded was our right to twinkle.

MARILYN MONROE

Dear reader,

We hope you enjoyed reading *Instead of Therapy*. Please take a moment to leave a review, even if it's a short one. Your opinion is important to us.

Discover more books by Rena Winters at https://www.nextchapter.pub/authors/rena-winters

Want to know when one of our books is free or discounted? Join the newsletter at http://eepurl.com/bqqB3H

Best regards,

Rena Winters and the Next Chapter Team

ABOUT THE AUTHOR

Multi-talented Rena Winters has enjoyed an outstanding career in the entertainment industry as a writer, talent, producer, production executive, and a major TV and Motion Picture executive.

Her writing ability won the coveted Angel Award for the "outstanding family TV special, **"How to Change Your Life,"** which she co-hosted with Robert Stack. She wrote the two-hour script (and co-produced) for **"My Little Corner of the World,"** winner of the Freedoms Foundation and American Family Heritage awards.

Feature films include **"The Boys Next Door," "KGB, the Secret War," "Charlie Chan & the Curse of the Dragon Queen,"** and **"Avenging Angel."**

Her producing credits include **"The Juliet Prowse Spectacular"** for 20th Century Fox, **"Sinatra - Las Vegas Style,"** and **"Peter Marshall - One More Time,"** which produced a best-selling soundtrack album.

As Executive Vice President, she headed the entire USA operation for the international entertainment giant, Sepp-Inter, producers of TV Series, TV Specials, Feature Films and all areas of merchandising for their animated entities, including **"The Smurfs," "Flipper," "Seabert," "The Snorks,"** and **"Foofur"** (all Emmy Award winners) plus **"After School Specials"** for CBS-TV.

Author of the bestselling book "**Smurfs: The Inside Story of the Little Blue Characters**" currently available on Amazon and Kindle and in all bookstores.

"**In Lieu of Therapy**," released October 2015, is an inspirational and uplifting easy reading book for busy people. Praised by the President of the American Authors Association as a must-read.

Contributing author to an anthology of patriots and heroes, "**I Pledge Allegiance**," sponsored by the Wednesday Warriors Writers group currently on Amazon and Kindle.

Latest book – "**Target One**" A story about how terrorism escalates in America. Winner 2nd Place Best Fiction 2018 by the Public Safety Writers Association.

Rena is a contributing writer to the "**summerlinww.blogspot.com**" as a member of the Summerlin Writers and Poets Group. She is also a contributing writer to WTTmagazine@gmail.com. She is a former writer/reporter for "**thenowreport.vegas**," an online newspaper.

In addition, Rena has recently completed writing a children's book featuring two rescue cats. She also has a forthcoming cookbook for people who don't have time to cook.

Rena Winters was voted one of the "50 Great Writers You Should Be Reading – 2017 and 2018" by The Authors Show.com.

At the College of Southern Nevada, Rena is an adjunct instructor teaching Creative Writing courses. She makes her home in Las Vegas, Nevada, and works in her spare time as an editor and ghostwriter.

Instead Of Therapy
ISBN: 978-4-86752-996-6

Published by
Next Chapter
1-60-20 Minami-Otsuka
170-0005 Toshima-Ku, Tokyo
+818035793528

3rd October 2021